SCHRIFTENREIHE
DES
FORSCHUNGSINSTITUTS FÜR EUROPAFRAGEN

WIRTSCHAFTS
UNIVERSITÄT

WIEN

BAND 13

EUROPEAN UNION: DEMOCRATIC PERSPECTIVES AFTER 1996

by

GERDA FALKNER
and
MICHAEL NENTWICH

SERVICE FACHVERLAG
Wien 1995

Die Deutsche Bibliotek – CIP-Einheitsaufnahme

Falkner, Gerda:
European Union : democratic perspectives after 1996 / by Gerda
Falkner and Michael Nentwich. – Wien : Service-Fachverl.,
1995
   (Schriftenreihe des Forschungsinstituts für Europafragen ; Bd. 13)
   ISBN 3-85428-346-6
NE: Nentwich, Michael:; Forschungsinstitut für Europafragen <Wien>:
   Schriftenreihe des Forschungsinstituts . . .

The Authors:
Vertr.-Ass. Mag. Dr. phil. *Gerda Falkner*, M.E.S. (Bruges)
Institute for State and Political Science,
University of Vienna
Hohenstaufengasse 9/7
A-1010 Vienna, Austria
email: a4361dab@helios.edvz.univie.ac.at

Univ.-Ass. Mag. Dr. iur. *Michael Nentwich*
Research Institute for European Affairs,
University of Economics and Business Administration Vienna
Althanstraße 39–45
A-1090 Vienna, Austria
email: nentwich@fgr.wu-wien.ac.at

Gefördert vom Bundesministerium für Wissenschaft
und Forschung in Wien

ISBN 3-85428-346-6

© Service Fachverlag, Wien
Druck: MANZ, 1050 Wien
Printed in Austria 1995

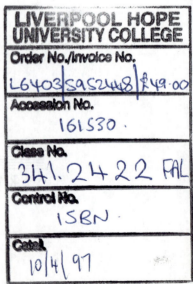

Preface

The present study aims at preparing the ground for an in-depth discussion of the highly salient issue of democratic reform of the European Union. This will be the major task of the next intergovernmental conference (IGC) which is due to start in 1996. However, it is very probable that the topic will stay on the European agenda for a much longer period.

We have collected a series of prominent contributions made in recent months with a view to the IGC. Clearly, we could not include all pertinent statements and publications but we assume that our collection covers all major contributions. There is also a bulk of secondary literature on the issue of how to solve the 'democratic deficit'. We shall present such contributions only occasionally, our main goal being to reflect the more fully-fledged or politically prominent proposals, and to assess the ongoing discussions. Therefore, this presentation together with our own proposals could serve as a rich quarry for ideas.

We would like to thank the Austrian Ministry for Science, Research and Arts which supported the study in the framework of the European Community Research Framework COST A7 'Democratic Rules for Europe' (Project N° GZ 20.805/2-II/2/94). We also want to express our gratitude to Professor *Jeremy Richardson* and the University of Essex (Department of Government), where major parts of this study were completed during our stay as Research Fellows under the Human Capital and Mobility Programme of the European Union. Last, but not least, many thanks to Professor *Stefan Griller*, who accepted our manuscript for publication in the series of the Research Institute for European Affairs.

Colchester, August 1995
Gerda Falkner
Michael Nentwich

Overview

Contents

Contents

Deutschsprachige Zusammenfassung (German Abstract)

Im Jahre 1996 wird eine neuerliche Regierungskonferenz der Mitgliedstaaten der Europäischen Union einberufen werden. Konkreter Anlaß sind einerseits die Überprüfung der Neuerungen, die durch den Maastrichter Vertrag eingeführt wurden, und andererseits die Herausforderungen, die sich der Union aufgrund der ins Auge gefaßten Ost- und Süderweiterungen stellen werden. Mittlerweile hat sich die Gesamtheit der Debattenbeiträge im Vorfeld der Konferenz zu einer regelrechten Europäischen Verfassungsdiskussion ausgeweitet, da verschiedene AutorInnen davon ausgehen, daß die anstehenden Probleme (Demokratie, Transparenz, Erweiterung, Effizienz) nur mehr durch eine Totalrevision des Vertragsgebäudes zu bewältigen sein werden.

Die vorliegende Studie hat es sich zum Ziel gesetzt, diese Debatte zu einem Zeitpunkt aufzuarbeiten, zu dem gleichsam die erste, noch informelle Runde der Vorbereitungen der Regierungskonferenz abgeschlossen ist und mit der formellen Einsetzung der sogenannten Reflexionsgruppe am 2. Juni 1995 bei einem EU Außenministertreffen in Messina eine nächste Phase begonnen wurde. Zum gegenwärtigen Zeitpunkt liegen nicht nur die Stellungnahmen aller Organe der Union zum Funktionieren des Vertrages über die Europäische Union sowie (teils) zu den Themen der Regierungskonferenz vor, sondern darüber hinaus etliche zum Teil sehr elaborierte Stellungnahmen von diversen Europäischen ExpertInnen, teils aus dem Umfeld der EU Organe, teils aus dem akademischen Bereich, sowie zahlreiche Wortmeldungen von nationalen PolitikerInnen und teilweise sogar von nationalen Organen (Parlamente, Regierungen). Darunter befinden sich auch zwei erst kürzlich veröffentlichte Verfassungsentwürfe, die den Diskurs nicht unwesentlich beeinflußt haben.

Die Studie ist wie folgt aufgebaut: in einem ersten Teil wird eine kurze Zustandsbeschreibung der institutionellen und verfahrensmäßigen Struktur der EU nach Maastricht gegeben, die insbesondere auch die Erfahrungen mit den neuen Bestimmungen aufgrund des Maastrichter Vertrages einbezieht (II.). Im anschließenden Teil werden die wesentlichsten Beiträge zur Reformdiskussion vor- und im Überblick dargestellt (III.A.). Der Hauptteil der Studie ist sodann der Diskussion der Hauptpunkte der vorraussichtlichen Tagesordnung der Regierungskonferenz gewidmet (III.B.).

Es wird zwischen strukturellen Fragen (III.B.1) einerseits, institutionellen Fragen (III.B.2.) und verfahrensmäßigen Fragen (III.B.3.) andererseits unterschieden. Zu den *strukturellen* Fragen gehören insbesondere die folgenden: Braucht die Union eine Verfassung? Wie kann der Integrationsprozeß flexibilisiert werden? Wie soll die zukünftige Kompetenzverteilung zwischen den Mitgliedstaaten und der EU geregelt werden? Und schließlich: Welche Rolle sollen die Europäischen BürgerInnen im Entscheidungsprozeß spielen? Unter der Überschrift *"Institutionelles"* wird folgendes erörtert: Wie sollen die Organe der EU zusammengesetzt sein? Welche Rolle soll das Europäische Parlament bei der Besetzung der anderen Organe spielen? Wie soll zukünftig die Präsidentschaft des Rates organisiert werden? Welche Rolle könnte der Regionalausschuß spielen? In welcher Beziehung sollen in Zukunft die nationalen Parlamente zum institutionellen System der EU stehen? Und schließlich: Welche Reformen sind im Bereich der Europäischen Gerichtsbarkeit vorstellbar? Das *Verfahrens*-Kapitel widmet sich abschließend organ-übergreifenden Fragen: Soll das Initiativmonopol der Kommission abgeschafft werden? In welcher Form ist das zukünftige EU-Rechtssetzungsverfahren vorzustellen? Insbesondere: Soll es in Zukunft ein einheitliches, möglicherweise sogar ein ausgefeiltes Zwei-Kammern-System geben? In welcher Weise ist eine Reform der Entscheidungserfordernisse im Rat vorstellbar? Hier geht es insbesondere um die mögliche Abschaffung der Einstimmigkeit und die ebenfalls durch zukünftige Erweiterungen reformbedürftige Qualifizierte Mehrheit. Weiters: In welcher Weise sollen sich, im Sinne der jüngst vieldiskutierten politischen Transparenz, die Beratungen im Rat öffnen? Welche Möglichkeiten gibt es, um die Implementierung von EG-Recht zu verbessern? Und schließlich: Wie sieht die Zukunft der Komitologie (also des unübersichtlichen Ausschußwesens bei der Umsetzung von Gemeinschaftspolitiken) aus?

In Anschluß an einen Problemaufriß und die Präsentation der in der laufenden Diskussion gemachten Lösungsvorschläge findet sich in jedem Unterkapitel ein Abschnitt, in dem die Frage aus einer spezifisch österreichischen Warte unter besonderer Berücksichtigung der demokratischen und föderalen Traditionen dieses Landes sowie seiner spezifischen politischen Lage beleuchtet wird. Hier werden eine Reihe von innovativen Vorschlägen eingebracht, welche angesichts der sich in der Diskussion abzeichnenden Probleme Lösungen präsentieren, die einen Bestandteil der zukünftigen österreichischen Verhandlungsposition darstellen könnten. Diese Vorschläge werden in Kapitel V. kurz gefaßt wiederholt.

Die Studie wird durch einige Thesen über die Perspektiven der demokratischen Reform abgerundet, die auf den im Hauptteil der Studie erörterten Lösungsansätzen und den sich abzeichnenden Ausgangspositionen der einzelnen Mitgliedsländer aufbauen (IV.).

I. Introduction

The so-called Maastricht Treaty or Treaty on European Union (TEU) provides, in its Article N (2), for an intergovernmental conference (IGC) in 1996 in order to revise a series of provisions[1]). These include, among others, the scope of the co-decision procedure and the issue of the hierarchy of Community acts. Since then it has become obvious that the agenda of the forthcoming IGC will be much wider. There are three main developments which inspire debate, public speech, the working of the EU institutions, and last but not least academic writing.

First, it turned out that the Maastricht Treaty did by no means resolve all institutional problems. The above-mentioned items postponed by the IGC 1991 for review in 1996 are but the tip of the iceberg. This became particularly obvious during the final phase of the negotiations leading to the 1995 enlargement when the so-called Ioannina compromise showed that the institutional structure had been stretched to its outer limits. Therefore, at various meetings held since the Treaty was signed, the European Council agreed to add more items to the list of topics to be considered. At its meeting in Brussels (10-11 December 1993) the following Declaration was published:

> "In adopting the institutional provisions of the Accession Treaty, the Member states and the applicant countries agree that, as well as examining the legislative role of the European Parliament and the other matters envisaged in the Treaty on European Union, the Intergovernmental Conference to be convened in 1996 will consider the questions relating to the number of members of the Commission and the weighting of the votes of the Member states in the Council. It will also consider any measures deemed necessary to facilitate the work of the Institutions and guarantee their effective operation."

The Corfu summit in June 1994 added that the preparation of the IGC would take place in a spirit of democracy and openness, with a view to further enlargement. Furthermore, the European Parliament (EP), the Council and the Commission agreed in the context of an inter-institutional agreement that two further matters be put on the agenda: the operation of budgetary procedures,

---

[1]) See Articles N (2), B dash 5, J.4 (6), J.10 EUT and 189b (8) ECT; Common Declaration N° 1 and 16 annexed to the Final Act.

notably as regards the classification of expenditure; and the arrangements for exercising the executive powers conferred on the Commission to implement legislation adopted under the co-decision procedure (comitology)[2]). A further 'constitutional' issue which has not yet been resolved is the ending of the Treaty establishing the European Coal and Steel Community in the year 2002[3]).

Second, the perspective of a Union further enlarged to the East and South made it clear that the institutional mechanisms designed for a Community of only six members which had so far only been adapted mechanically without changing the original principles, would not match up with the needs of a Union of some 28 Member states. Therefore, the European Council put the topic of "appropriate institutional arrangements to ensure that the Union will operate smoothly in the event of enlargement to include Cyprus, Malta and the countries of Central and Eastern Europe" on the agenda[4]).

Third, during the difficult ratification process of the Maastricht Treaty (February 1992 until October 1993)[5]), it became obvious that the "Maastricht Union" marked a still unsatisfactory stage of the institutional development at the Euro-level. The pertinent issue of the democratic deficit and lacking legitimacy of the Union's decision-making structure, as well as the call for more transparency in the workings of the institutions, and the question of subsidiarity and hence the division of competencies/powers between the Union and its Member states were highlighted during numerous debates at both European and national levels, including the new Member states.

Over the last two years, these three developments converged into a genuine constitutional debate, and it might well be that the negotiations during the next IGC in 1996 will lead to a qualitative leap in the development of the Union. There are not only a series of innovative proposals with respect to specific problems but also two major and comprehensive proposals for a European

---

[2]) OJ 93/C 331.

[3]) See Article 97 of this Treaty.

[4]) See the conclusions of the Brussels and Corfu summits in December 1993 and June 1994.

[5]) See especially the necessity of a second referendum in Denmark, the slight majority in the French referendum, and the constitutional dispute in Germany.

Constitution in 1993 and 1994[6]). Still, some two years ahead of its closing date, it is clearly inappropriate to venture a prediction of what the outcome of the IGC 1996 might be. However, the end of the first informal stage of the preparation of the IGC seems to be a convenient moment for summarising the debate and assessing the democratic perspectives of the Union after 1996.

At the Corfu European Council in June 1994, it was decided that a "reflection group" be in charge of preparing the IGC. The task assigned to the Reflection Group by the Council of Corfu is to examine and develop ideas concerning the provisions of the Maastricht Treaty whose revisions are scheduled, and concerning other possible improvements, in a spirit of democracy and openness, on the basis of reports by the institutions on the functioning of the TEU[7]). This, together with the above-mentioned formal amendment of the IGC's agenda, marked the starting point for intensive debate and reflection on the reform of the institutional system of the EU. Meanwhile some Member states' governments or representatives made their first contributions and the academic world started to take on the issue. The Corfu summit also gave a mandate to the Community institutions to review the operation of the Treaty on European Union. Consequently, a series of reports on the institutions' experiences with the Maastricht Treaty were published between March and May 1995 (see III.A.1).

The EP, in its report to the Reflection Group, called for as open a debate as possible during the preparation of the IGC. It asked for an opportunity to participate in the negotiations and to give its assent to the outcome. The first part of this request, which had been repeated on numerous occasions without success before the last two IGCs, was accepted by the Member states: two representatives of the Parliament take part in the deliberations of the Reflection Group. The EP has also proposed a large hearing on the issues at stake (which is obviously meant to be public); consultative conferences of parliaments at the beginning and end of the revision conference; and a Union-wide referendum to ratify any Treaty provisions, "on the grounds that a collective decision affecting the whole of Europe is at stake"[8]). The former proposal has not been

---

[6]) European Constitutional Group 1993, Herman Report 1994, see below III.A.2.a and III.A.2.g.

[7]) See Council, Projet de Rapport sur le Fonctionnement du Traité sur L'Union Européenne, SN 1821/95, 14 March 1995, 1.

[8]) EP Resolution from 17. 5. 1995, PE 190.441, pt. 41 ff.

taken up so far, whereas the idea of a referendum has been voiced by politicians on a number of occasions[9]).

The Reflection Group was set up formally at the meeting of the General Affairs Council on 2 June 1995 in Messina[10]). Thus, the second and more formal stage of the preparation of the IGC has just begun. The Group will meet regularly and is required to present a formal report to the European Council in Madrid in December 1995. Based on the Group's report this summit will then set up the official agenda of the IGC. It will be the task of the next Presidency (Italy) to convene the Conference during the first half of 1996. For tactical reasons it might well be that the Conference could either start rather late or last longer than 1996; there is little chance that the final political decisions will be taken before the British elections (at the latest in April 1997).

The following study assesses the prospects for democratic reform of the European Union. For this purpose we shall first look at the present state of democracy at the supranational level. In this respect a first assessment of the working of the new provisions, especially of the so-called co-decision procedure, seems particularly interesting. We shall look into the evidence of some one-and-a-half years of experience with the newest elaborate decision-making procedure which has been designed by the last IGC: the co-decision modus. We shall then go on to present the major contributions to the ongoing debate on institutional/constitutional reform. Their authors are either the EU institutions, individual members of the Brussels in-group, (groups of) academics, or Member states politicians. In a third step we shall then discuss the key issues of the debate. In this respect we distinguish between structural, institutional and procedural issues. After each presentation of a key issue we shall present a genuine Austrian perspective. In the Conclusions we try to evaluate the prospects of democratic reform after 1996.

---

[9])   E.g. *W. Martens*, MEP, proposed such a constitutional referendum which should take place the same day in all Member states of the Union (Agence Europe, 3/4. October 1994, 2).

[10])   Its members are two MEPs, *E. Brok* and *E. Guigou*; one Commissioner, *M. Oreja Aguirre* (the former Institutional Affairs Committee rapporteur of the EP); and the fifteen representatives of the Member states: the Spaniard *C. Westendorp* as the head of the group, *N. Ersbøll* (Dm), *W. Hoyer* (FRG), *S. Stathanos* (Gr), *G. Mitchell* (Irl), *S. Fagiolo* (It), *J. Weyland* (Lux), *M. Patijn* (Ne), *M. Scheich* (A), *A. G. Pereira* (P), *I. Melin* (SF), *G. Lund* (S), *D. Davis* (UK), *J. de Bock* (Be), *M. Barnier* (F).

II. The Status Quo of Democracy at the EU Level

A. *The Development of Existing Institutions and Procedures*

When European integration was founded in the 1950s, it was clearly not the dimension of democracy which caught the attention of the 'spiritus rector' Monnet and his fellows. Only tactical considerations made them include a parliamentary assembly in the new European Coal and Steel Community:

> "Since there was already the rather large assembly of the Council of Europe, the founding fathers of the new Community thought it might be safer to include a new parliamentary body in their plans, thus excluding all possible attempts from the Council of Europe Assembly to fill the gap and to exercise parliamentary control of the ECSC."[11]

The competent institutions within the ECSC were the High Authority composed of (originally six) appointed members, and the Council consisting of representatives of the governments. The assembly, in contrast, had no legislative function whatsoever but purely "supervisory" character (see Article 20 ECSC-Treaty). Within the European Economic Community (EEC), established in 1957, the Council of Ministers was even strengthened vis-à-vis the Commission in order to prevent criticism regarding supranational aspects, especially in France. The control functions granted to the Assembly, such as the right to question, to debate the annual general report on the activities of the Community, and to table a motion of censure, were all targeted at the Commission and hence not at the main decision-taking body, i.e. the Council. Contrasting the development of the Economic and Social Committee (ESC) consisting of representatives of various professions and economic interests, the EEC Assembly, however, managed to considerably increase its powers and legitimacy over time. This process relied on formal (Treaty amendments) as well as informal foundations (such as so-called inter-institutional agreements between the EC institutions). First, in 1976 it was finally decided to switch from a system of indirect representation to direct election of MEPs. Since the first elections in 1979, Parliament has been based on improved (formal) legitimacy. Second, being the result of bargaining on a case to case basis, improvements in the Parliament's 'powers' were introduced. However, they varied among policy

---

[11] *Neunreither 1995, 1.*

areas and followed no single procedural logic. Thus, there were at least five major categories of powers for the EP (each including diverse sub-procedures) already in force before the Maastricht Treaty:

The *consultation* procedure implies that the Council ultimately has to wait for the parliamentarians' opinion in order to legislate according to the governments' ideas. So-called *concertation* was introduced for legislative acts with significant budgetary consequences, in case no other form of EP participation be provided for in the Treaties[12]). The *co-operation* procedure was introduced by the Single European Act 1986 in order to facilitate adoption of the many legislative acts within the internal market programme: in some cases where the Council may potentially act by a qualified majority, the EP has the power to first give an opinion on a project, and then, in a second reading, to possibly reject the Council's Common Position. In such a case, the Council may still adopt its text — though only by unanimity (for details see Article 189c ECT). In cases where the EP suggests amendments to the Council's Common Position, the Commission is crucial: only amendments backed by it may be adopted without a unanimity requirement[13]). Within the EC's complicated *budgetary procedure*, in contrast, the EP disposes of stronger powers, as it has the final authority over the so-called 'non-obligatory' expenses. Finally, adhesion and association treaties already needed the formal *assent* of the European Parliament before the TEU entered into force. The latter has somewhat extended the scope of this procedure, also to the appointment of the Commission President; specific questions concerning the European Central Bank; citizenship; the uniform electoral procedure; certain international agreements; and reform decisions within the structural funds policies.

The major innovation of the Maastricht Treaty, however, was the new and additional procedure of *co-decision* between Council and Parliament (see Article 189b ECT). In the second and third readings, the EP ultimately has a veto power: if it rejects the proposal by an absolute majority of its members, the project has failed. The detailed procedural rules, however, look far more complicated than this. There may, for example, be a Conciliation Committee convened if the EP announces that it might veto the proposal. This committee

---

[12]) This model was introduced by a Common Declaration of Council, Commission, and EP (4 March 1975; OJ 75/C 89/1).

[13]) This has since the outset been a major point of criticism concerning the co-operation procedure.

consists of an equal number of representatives of both the Council and the EP, who for the first time in EC history are forced to directly negotiate with each other. Any outcome of this committee may be approved by an absolute majority in the EP and (normally) by qualified majority within the Council. If there is no consensus to be found in the Conciliation Committee, the Council may still adopt its Common Position by (normally) a qualified majority within six weeks. In cases where the EP does not veto within another six weeks, the act is deemed adopted. This new decision-making procedure applies — sometimes not exclusively, however — in the fields of free movement of workers (Article 49 ECT), right of establishment [Articles 54 (2); 56 (2); 57 (1); 57 (2) 3rd sentence], services (Article 66), internal market (Articles 100a, 100b), education (Article 126), culture (Article 128), health (Article 129), consumers (Article 129a), trans-European networks (Article 129d), and environment [Article 130s (3)][14].

The major criticisms voiced against the Maastricht compromises are as follows: First, the existing gaps in parliamentary control were not consequently eliminated, as there were still many decisions with majority vote (so that national parliamentary scrutiny falls short) but without co-decision by the EP, so that possible decisions against the will of both national and European parliaments were not consequently excluded. Second, the EP was completely kept outside the management of important additional Union competencies in the fields of common foreign and security policy (CFSP) as well as justice and home affairs (JHA). Third, the new procedure, also generally welcomed as to its implications on EP powers, was criticised for being too complicated and potentially time consuming (see below II.B.1). Fourth, co-decision was simply added to the considerable amount of other procedures which already existed, thus increasing the total number of variants and adding to the lack of transparency vis-à-vis the citizens. Finally, the range of questions where co-decision was agreed to apply follows no evident structural logic (as is also true partly for other procedures). For example, there are two cases where even co-decision and requirement of unanimity are combined (i.e. in the fields of culture and research, Articles 128 and 130l ECT).

Despite the fact that, perhaps to the surprise of many, the co-decision procedure is in general described by the EC institutions to have worked quite satisfactorily so far (see below II.B.1), it is thus no wonder that the debate for a

---

[14]) See Council document SN 1823/95, OR.F, Annex V, F 12.

more democratic and transparent set-up for the European Union has never waned.

B. Assessment of the Working of the Maastricht Treaty's New Provisions

The institutions' reports on the functioning of the Maastricht Treaty assess a broad range of new provisions and policies. We shall deal here only with those which have an impact on the institutional and procedural dimension of the Union and, thus, on democracy.

1. Co-decision

Although co-decision has only been applied for just over one and a half years, there is already considerable experience in the field because the procedure covers approximately 25 % of the legislative activity of the Community[15]). By May 1995, 136 proposals for co-decision acts had been forwarded to Parliament; in the case of 30 proposals, the procedure was terminated; Parliament received 33 common positions, in 18 cases agreement between Council and EP had been reached without convening the Conciliation Committee; in 13 cases approval of a joint text by the Committee was approved; in one of these cases (the biotechnology patents Directive) the plenary did not follow the delegation's recommendations. This fact has undermined the whole process in the eyes of the Council[16]). Only once was the Conciliation Committee unable to agree on a joint text (the voice telephony Directive); in that case the Council confirmed its common position, which was nevertheless subsequently rejected by Parliament[17]). The average length of the procedure was less than 300 days which is "fairly quickly" in the eyes of the Commission[18]).

In his assessment, *Miller* comes to the conclusion that the role of the Commission has radically changed: while it was the intermediary between the

---

[15]) *G. Miller*, "Post-Maastricht Legislative Procedures: Is the Council 'Institutionally Challenged'?", paper presented to the 4th Biennial International Conference of ECSA in Charleston, South Carolina, 11-14 May 1995 (Miller 1995), 10. *Gary Miller* is a Parliament official in the Conciliations Secretariat.

[16]) Council document SN 1821/95, pt. 24.

[17]) *Miller* 1995, 10 f.

[18]) Commission Report, SEC(95) 731, 19.

Council and the EP under the old co-operation procedure, Parliament now negotiates directly with the Council:

> "Although the Treaty states (...) that the Commission 'shall take all the necessary initiatives with a view to reconciling the positions of the European Parliament and the Council', during the conciliation exercise the Commission is *de facto* no longer able to withdraw its proposal and its legal right to do so is the subject of dispute. Moreover, any amendments which it might propose do not affect the majorities required in the Committee. In practice, in the majority of cases, compromise proposals have originated in either the Council or Parliament delegations."[19]

However, the Commission comes to the conclusion that "[c]ontrary to certain fears resulting from its complexity and its length, the co-decision procedure has worked well so far"[20] and does not challenge it in principle.

Obviously, there was considerable divergence between the two main actors concerning the actual operation of the Conciliation Committee. Parliament took the view that the Committee is "an inter-institutional body laid down in the Treaty with considerable autonomy to organise its own work as it sees fit and to make its own decisions"[21]. In contrast, the Council does not share this view of the Committee's autonomy, therefore the composition of the Council's delegation varies considerably: the President-in-office is always a minister, but usually the other national delegations are represented by COREPER I. Since "Ministers are more capable of delivering compromises", this situation is "far from being satisfactory" for MEPs who, "as elected representatives, often find it a frustrating experience to try and negotiate with unelected diplomats who may be operating under an extremely limited mandate from their governments"[22]. On the other hand, *Miller* reports that the proceedings in the Committee are far from being real conciliation deliberations, since the members of each delegation have a very different view of their role in the Committee:

> "Whenever possible compromises are explored this means that, as soon as they develop the concrete form of a proposed text, Council

---

[19] *Miller* 1995, 17.

[20] Commission Report, SEC(95) 731, 19.

[21] *Miller* 1995, 19.

[22] *Miller* 1995, 20.

9

always has to ask for the proceedings to be suspended to allow its delegations to consult, the Presidency being unable to speak on their behalf in respect of the new text and unwilling for Council to be seen deliberating or even voting on the proposals in front of the MEPs. (...) frequently a large number of interruptions are needed before a compromise is reached. (...) This makes for an inefficient use of negotiating time and an unnecessary proliferation of meetings."[23]

Given the cumbersome procedure, the inflexible deadlines imposed by the Treaty and the Council's difficulty with negotiating in the formal setting of the Conciliation Committee, the importance of informal negotiating mechanisms has grown. At (meanwhile) regular informal trialogue meetings, attended by the chairman and rapporteur of the responsible EP committee, the chairman of COREPER and the Commissioner responsible, possible compromises are being explored[24].

In its report to the Reflection Group the Council concludes that "co-decision could be considered as generally satisfying"[25]. Nevertheless, it made some critical points: it raised for example the question of the "contractual capacity" of Parliament's delegation to the Conciliation Committee in its relation to the plenary. It also criticised Parliament's linking of its assent with other questions such as comitology and the fact that the parliamentarians in the Conciliation Committee sometimes take up again amendments which were previously voted down by the plenary in second reading[26].

Although the overall experience seems to be positive[27], there seems to be agreement that the procedure as laid down in Article 189b ECT is "imprecise on a number of points"[28] and "overly-complex"[29]. Therefore, reform of the procedure along the lines of simplification and clarification might be a common

---

[23] *Miller* 1995, 21.

[24] *Miller* 1995, 24.

[25] Council Report, SN 1821/95, pt. 19.

[26] Council Report, SN 1821/95, pt. 24.

[27] Council Report, SN 1821/95, pt. 19; Commission Report, SEC(95) 731, 43; EP Resolution from 17. 5. 1995, PE 190.441, pt. 29 ff.; *Miller* 1995, 30.

[28] Commission Report, SEC(95) 731, 23 f.

[29] *Miller* 1995, 18; see also Council Report, SN 1821/95, pt. 24; EP Resolution from 17. 5. 1995, PE 190.441, pt. 30.

denominator in the forthcoming IGC (see below III.B.3.b.3). From a political point of view *Miller* draws the general conclusion that the co-decision procedure be

> "fundamentally different in nature from the co-operation procedure: it involves a common act of the Council and Parliament. Throughout the procedure leading to the adoption of the act, the two institutions are on an equal footing. Parliament no longer has to give an 'opinion' which the Council, deciding on its own, may or may not take into account. It participates fully in legislative decisions."[30])

2. Parliament's Involvement in Appointments

Since the entry into force of the TEU, Parliament was involved in several appointments concerning the President of the new European Monetary Institute, members of the Court of Auditors, and, most interestingly, the new *Santer* Commission at the beginning of 1995.

In the *Commission's* view, the new approval procedure has proved "a highly convincing exercise" for three reasons: first, it gives it a "firm grounding of legitimacy"; second, it serves to "encourage greater dialogue" between Commission and Parliament; third, it "generates public interest"[31]). The only critical remark in the Commission's report relates to the lengthiness of the whole process (ibid.). This is also the starting point of a (however not further elaborated) critical remark by the *Council,* which later on concludes that the dependence of the Commission on Parliament could affect the institutional balance[32]).

During and after the hearing, the EP raised a series of criticisms concerning some of the nominated Commissioners (P. Flynn and the three Scandinavian candidates) and the distribution of portfolios. Then President-designate *Santer* "made a few additional gestures towards the Parliament, including taking away the chairmanship of the Commission working group on equal opportunities from Mr. *Flynn* and reserving it for himself", "clarified a number of uncertain points concerning the distribution of competencies", and made some "vaguer promises" concerning the forthcoming new Code of Conduct between the

---

[30]) *Miller* 1995, 30.

[31]) Commission Report, SEC(95) 731, 12.

[32]) Council Report, SN 1821/95, pt. 30.

Commission and the Parliament[33]). On this basis the plenary of the EP then voted to approve the new Commission. From the subsequent meetings specially devoted to the new procedures *F. Jacobs*, a senior official in the Secretariat General of the EP, reports that general satisfaction was expressed[34]).

As to Parliament's consultative involvement in the appointment of the President of the European Monetary Institute, *Jacobs* argues that it was a success because, first, EP resisted successfully the pressure to give its opinion within only a few days as urged by the Council, and second, the nominee (*A. Lamfalussy*) agreed to appear before Parliament's responsible committee (a requirement that had been laid down in the EP's Rules of Procedure but was not in the Treaty) and to answer written questions[35]). Finally, Parliament approved the nomination. On the other hand, *Jacobs* describes the involvement in the nominations to the European Court of Auditors as "a less satisfactory experience": first, the Council had given Parliament "unrealistic deadlines" and had concealed from it some information forwarded by the national authorities in reply to a specific request from the EP; second, despite the EP's rejection of two nominees since the entry into force of the TEU, the Council nevertheless appointed them[36]).

3. Selected Further Provisions

a) Voting rights in another Member state: The right of European citizens to vote and stand in elections outside their Member state of origin (see Article 8b ECT) was regulated with regard to the European elections in a Council Directive shortly after the entry into force of the TEU[37]), and also local elections in another Directive which is to be transposed in national law by the end of 1995[38]).

---

[33]) *Francis Jacobs*, "The European Parliament's Role in Nominating the Members of the Commission (...)", paper prepared for the 4th Biennial International Conference of ECSA in Charleston, South Carolina, 11-14 May 1995 (Jacobs 1995), 14; *Jacobs* is an official in the EP General Secretariat.

[34]) *Jacobs* 1995, 15.

[35]) *Jacobs* 1995, 7.

[36]) *Jacobs* 1995, 8 f.

[37]) OJ 93/L 329/34.

[38]) OJ 94/L 368/38.

In the Commission's 1996 report the following critical remark with respect to local elections is to be found:

> "[T]he citizen enjoys only fragmented, incomplete rights which are themselves subject to restrictive conditions. In that sense, the concept of citizenship is not yet put into practice in a way that lives up to the individual's expectations."[39]

b) Committee of the Regions: From April 1994 until February 1995, the CoR has been asked for sixteen opinions by the Council, six by the Commission, and has delivered ten opinions on its own initiative[40]. The issues covered by these opinions range from the Regulations establishing the Cohesion Fund and the Action Programme SOCRATES, to the Bathing Water Directive, the TGV Directive, and the Initiative URBAN.

The Commission — referring to the Committee's own-initiative opinion relating to clearance of the accounts of the CAP — seems to be of the opinion that the Committee of the Regions "may be running the risk of casting its net too wide"[41]. The Council states in its report that the definition of the details of the common organisational structure with the Economic and Social Committee (ESC), as provided in Protocol N° 16 annexed to the TEU, "has raised some difficulties"[42]; this is also mentioned in the CoR's report (see III.A.1.e).

c) Ombudsperson: The Committee of Petitions and the plenary of the EP have so far not been able to reach compromise on the electoral procedure for appointing the first Ombudsperson[43], which is a "regrettable fact"[44].

d) EP's Right to Request a Proposal From the Commission: Up to May 1995, Parliament has twice made use of this new right, first concerning the prevention and remedy of damage to the environment, and second, concerning hotel safety. "These requests are being considered by the Commission"[45].

---

[39] Commission Report, SEC(95) 731, 10.

[40] Council Report, SN 1823/95, Annex VI.

[41] Commission Report, SEC(95) 731, 15.

[42] Council Report, SN 1821/95, pt. 34.

[43] The compromise reached in October 1993 (see N° 159 of the Parliament's Rules of Procedures) was put into question by the newly elected Parliament in 1994.

[44] Commission Report, SEC(95) 731 final, 10.

[45] Commission Report, SEC(95) 731 final, 14.

III.   The Current Reform Debate

In this part of the report we shall proceed in two steps. First, we present the main proposals made during the run up for the IGC '96 as to end of June 1995 (A). Second, we elaborate on the key issues which have emerged so far (B).

A. The Main Proposals

The concepts proposed with a view to the IGC '96 can be roughly divided into three main groups according to authorship: those made by the EU institutions, those made by representatives of governments of single Member states, and those put forward by others, primarily by groups related to the academic world and dedicated to contributing to this reform debate. Please note that the following presentation of the major proposals concentrates on their main features (background, character and main contents) only. *A more detailed analysis (along with references to other contributors to the debate) being provided in the next section which discusses the single key issues of institutional reform within the IGC 1996.*

1. Contributions by EU Institutions

As reported in the introduction, the Corfu European Council in June 1994 decided that a "reflection group" should be in charge of preparing the forthcoming IGC. Accordingly, the Corfu summit also gave a mandate to the Community institutions to review the operation of the Treaty on European Union, in order to facilitate the work of this group. Therefore, a series of reports on the institutions' experiences with the Maastricht Treaty were presented during late spring 1995. These reports vary: some of them only discuss a few limited matters (such as the reports of the two Courts), while others, for example the Commission's report, are very detailed and include some broader aspects of the future development of the Union, such as further enlargement, and some substantive policy areas such as EMU. In the following section, however, we shall concentrate only on those proposals made with a view to institutional reform, while omitting equally interesting remarks with respect to the content of policies.

a) The Commission

On 10 May 1995 the Commission presented its 'Report on the Operation of the Treaty on European Union'[46]. As the title suggests, this text presents a careful assessment of the developments since the entry into force of the Maastricht Treaty. furthermore, a number of specific improvements are suggested.

As pointed out in the preface, the Commission considers the two major challenges for the Union to be, first, "to make Europe the business of every citizen", and second, to make "a success of future enlargement". In order to meet these challenges, the Commission goes on to suggest a two-fold objective for the IGC: increasing democracy as well as effectiveness. Consequently the report has two main parts: the first focuses on "Democracy and Transparency in the Union", the second on "Effectiveness and Consistency of the Union's Policies". The latter deals mainly with an operational assessment of the Union's activities in its three pillars. Although we acknowledge the importance of the actual outcome of the Union's decision-making processes in terms of social legitimacy, the analysis of specific policy areas lies beyond the remit of our study.

With respect to the institutional balance, the Commission judges its own role to be crucial and indispensable within the institutional system. It urges that its exclusive right of initiative be preserved (p. 3). It asks for a "fundamental text which [the European citizens] can invoke as a summary of their rights and duties" (p. 4). The Commission also believes that the EP should have the right to give its assent to any amendment to the Treaties. It furthermore advocates a wider use of the majority rule and argues that different speeds of integration should be possible, provided that this happens within a single institutional framework and centres on a common objective (p. 6).

With regard to the decision-making procedures, the Commission advocates not only more precision in the wording of Article 189b ECT but also simplification of the procedural rules and more logical criteria with respect to the applicability of the various legislative procedures as a whole (p. 23 f).

Furthermore, the Commission's report asks for the introduction of effective control measures (extended legal bases and instruments) in order to fight fraud more effectively (p. 28). Concerning transparency, it considers the dilution of the provision which allows for a Council decision against making voting results

---

[46] SEC(95) 731 final.

15

public (p. 32), and finally suggests the merging of the three Communities and the Union, as well as the Union's basic treaties, into single entities (p. 34).

b) The EP (Bourlanges/Martin Report)

The EP report on the 1996 IGC constitutes the Parliament's mandate for the two representatives in the Reflection Group on the IGC (i.e. *Elmar Brok*, EPP/Germany and *Elisabeth Guigou*, Socialist/France). Compared to former input by the primary representatives of the European citizens at supranational level (see e.g. the Herman Report, below), this report contains few far-reaching proposals for institutional reform. In the words of the draft report's authors (*Jean-Louis Bourlanges*, EPP/France and *David Martin*, Socialist/UK)[47]), the EP has shown "excessive timidity on some points"[48]), and respectively has "adopted a pragmatic and constructive attitude"[49]). The final version of the report was the subject of considerable controversy within the EP, including disputes within fractions, and among the two rapporteurs on major issues such as lifting all unanimity requirements (in the end, unanimity remained for constitutional matters and Article 235) and the question of a European constitution (despite all requests of its predecessors, the recently elected EP asks only for a Treaty between the governments). After having voted on 225 amendments in the plenary[50]), the EP finally adopted its 'Resolution on the functioning of the Treaty on European Union with a view to the 1996 Intergovernmental Conference — Implementation and development of the Union' on 17 May 1995 by 289 yes, 103 no and 74 abstentions[51]). However, the EP announced that its definitive position would not be adopted until February or March 1996, i.e. shortly before the beginning of the IGC[52]).

The resolution points out that the IGC '96 will have to face up to a "threefold institutional challenge": (1) the democratic deficit which a growing number of citizens find unacceptable"; (2) the "excessively complex and cumber-

---

[47]) On behalf of the Committee on Institutional Affairs, *Jean-Louis Bourlanges* and *David Martin* presented their consolidated report on 4 May 1995 (A4-0102/95).

[48]) *Bourlanges*, cited from Agence Europe, 19 May 1995, 2.

[49]) *Martin*, cited from Agence Europe, 19 May 1995, 2.

[50]) For details see Agence Europe, 18 May 1995, 2 ff.

[51]) See protocol of EP's session on 17 May 1995, PE 190.441; Agence Europe, 18 May 1995, 5.

[52]) Agence Europe, 22 June 1995, 4.

some and often inefficient" decision-making processes; and (3) the preparation for future enlargement without slowing and watering down the integration process. The lack of openness and accountability of the Council, and institutional mechanisms designed for a Europe of six Member states only, were the major deficiencies as established by the EP in the area under scrutiny here.

The EP's guidelines include the option of a merger of the three pillars and a single institutional framework (pt. 1), as well as the gradual integration of what is now the third pillar and the Schengen agreement (pt. 4). However, "specific features of the former 'pillars' could be retained for certain items over a predetermined transitional period" (pt. 14.i). Although the EP is strongly opposed to a 'Europe à la carte', it accepts "further flexible arrangements" under certain conditions which for example include the EP's overall responsibility[53]) for exercising control over those Union policies which are pursued by a limited number of Member states on a temporary basis (pt. 16).

In order to tackle the persistent problem of the democratic deficit the Parliament asks — as in previous contributions — to be attributed equal status with the Council in all fields of EU legislation and budgetary competence (pt. 23.iii). In addition, the EP wants to strengthen national parliaments in the process of European integration by involving them in the framework of joint sessions of respective parliamentary committees and by giving them a greater role with respect to the ministers before the latter vote in the Council on any major issue (pt. 24). The EP seeks to reduce the number of decision-making procedures to three: assent (restricted to 'constitutional matters'); consultation (in the field of CFSP only); and, as the general rule, co-decision. Furthermore the co-decision procedure should be simplified (pt. 29 f.).

Finally, the EP calls for as open a debate as possible during the preparation of the IGC and makes some specific proposals in that regard (pt. 41 ff., see above I.).

c) The Council

The Council of Ministers released its 'Report on the Functioning of the Treaty on European Union' on 20 April 1995[54]). The Council's report is pri-

---

[53]) Acting as a whole, i.e. not excluding MEPs from states which are not participating in the specific policy area.

[54]) Document 5082/1/95. We cite from a previous draft circulated as Document SN 1821/95 OR.F from 14 March 1995.

marily thought to be 'neutral'. As the authors in the Council's Secretariat General state in the introduction, they aim at a pure description of how the TEU's innovations worked out, without any predictions, judgements of values, or even suggestions to the reflection group.

The report has six parts: the first a general one, the second on citizenship, the third on the institutional system, one part on the Community's competencies, and two on the second and third pillars respectively. It is completed by a 50 page annex containing partly very innovative and interesting information, for example on the open sessions of the Council; statistical material relating to the application of the different legislative procedures; the use of Article 235 ECT; the CFSP and JHA activities etc.

The chapter on the institutional system is only eight pages long and starts with the remarkable sentence:

> "The decisions have to be taken at the Union level under conditions which are as democratic as those prevailing at the Member states' level." (pt. 15, our translation from French)

The report then goes on to stress the double aim of reinforcement of democratic legitimacy, and improvement of efficiency as the yardsticks for evaluation of the functioning of the Maastricht Treaty. It is suggested that the democratic legitimacy of the Union could not be based on the role of the European Parliament alone, but has to be the expression of the whole of the institutional system which cannot be compared with the national systems. The report repeats the well-known argument that the Council, although not subject to the EP's control, guarantees no less the respect of the democratic functioning of the system, because its members are politically responsible vis-à-vis their national parliaments (pt. 17). The Council seems to be satisfied with co-decision and with the extension of qualified majority voting. However, it points out that relatively few decisions are actually taken by majority voting because the eventuality of being in the minority proves to be a good incentive to search for necessary compromises (pt. 18 f.). The Council criticises Parliament's "tendency to interpret widely and, occasionally, to overstep its competencies" (pt. 21, our translation), and therefore concludes that the first months of application of the TEU were characterised by persisting institutional conflicts (pt. 33). The Council's remarks on the functioning of co-decision with the EP are quite critical concerning certain details, but remain positive in the overall assessment (see above II.B.1). With respect to the new procedure of appointing the

Commission, the report argues that the EP's involvement enhanced the Commission's dependence on the Parliament and therefore affected the institutional balance (pt. 30). The Council is opposed to further inter-institutional agreements with the Parliament (pt. 32).

d) The European Courts

The European Court of Justice (ECJ) presented its 'Report on Certain Aspects of the Application of the Treaty on European Union' in May 1995, and the Court of First Instance (CFI) its 'Contribution with a View to the IGC 1996' on 17 May 1995[55]). The Courts restrict their reports to the role of the jurisdiction in the European Union and therefore do not contribute to most of the major issues at stake in the IGC 1996.

The *ECJ* sees itself as a "constitutional court" of the Union (pt. 3) and wants this role to be preserved (pt. 4). It calls for extension of its authority to review Union activities in the fields of the second and third pillars (pt. 4). In general, the ECJ is of the opinion that the judicial structure of the Union should not be altered at the present stage of development (pt. 15). Most of the difficulties, such as the diminishing but still considerable time-lag between filing a case to the Court and its final decision, could be solved by internal measures. The ECJ is opposed to further increasing the number of judges because of its character as a collegiate but acknowledges the problem of representation of further Member states (pt. 16). It is against hearings in the EP before the appointment of judges (pt. 17). Finally the Court considers the IGC '96 to be a good opportunity to codify and settle the Union's basic texts (pt. 23).

The *CFI's* report concentrates on different ways to improve its work based on experiences of the past few years. In this respect only minor Treaty amendments are suggested because the necessary provisions could be made on the basis of its internal organisational powers: it is opposed to the creation of regional or specialised courts (p. 5) but suggests the introduction of single judges and/or specialised chambers for certain categories of cases, auxiliary rapporteurs, and an increase in the number of judges of the CFI (p. 6 ff.). With respect to appointment procedures and the term of office, there are some differences in the options of the ECJ: the Court of First Instance is not opposing any participation of the EP in the appointment of judges, but suggests that

---

[55]) Both documents do not have any specific reference number and are laid out and printed in the same way as the Courts decisions, before they are reported in the Court Series.

it be restricted to their first term of office; in order to secure continuity of the work of the Court it favours the possibility of re-appointment (p. 9 ff.); finally it asks for the appropriate inclusion in the Treaty text and to be named among the institutions in Article 4 (2) ECT (p. 11 f).

e) The Committee of the Regions

The CoR adopted on 20 April 1995, almost unanimously [one vote against, four abstentions[56])], its 'Opinion on the Revision of the Treaty on European Union'[57]), based on the so-called *Pujol report*. The Opinion also includes in annex a supplementary Opinion in the Union from 4 May 1995 which elaborates on the CoR's assessment of the working of the subsidiarity principle. The report and resolution suggest improvements to the Maastricht Treaty concerning local and regional participation. The proposals are sometimes quite far-reaching, despite the fact that after lively debate no legislative functions were requested, and the controversial question of dividing the Committee into two sub-units, representing the regional and local governments respectively, was dropped. The CoR only wants to increase the cases where an opinion by it be obligatory, and that the Union legislator be required to give the reasons in cases where it does not follow the CoR's opinion (p. 8).

The CoR sees itself as one pillar of democratic legitimacy of the Union (p. 3). The report proposes a rewording of Article 3b ECT (principle of subsidiarity) so that regional and local authorities be specifically mentioned alongside the Member states[58]). This principle should be complemented by a specific catalogue of Union competencies (p. 5). It also asks that the ECJ should have the jurisdiction in actions brought by the CoR against the violation of the principle of subsidiarity as well as in actions brought by the regions whose legislative powers might be affected by EC law (p. 5). The Committee wants to be formally recognised as an EC institution, and to see its consultative functions extended to all areas where consultation is provided for the ESC; to development co-operation policy; Union citizenship; and state aid. In order to increase

---

[56]) See Agence Europe, 24 April 1995, 4.

[57]) CdR 136/95 (SP) HB/M/CW/R/ms.

[58]) The Community should intervene "only if and in so far as the objectives of the proposed action cannot be sufficiently achieved by Member states, or by the regional and local authorities endowed with powers under the domestic legislation of the Member state in question."

its legitimacy the Committee wants Article 198a ECT to be amended so that in future its members would need to have a mandate from the electorate or to be politically accountable to an assembly elected by universal suffrage. Finally, it requests full organisational and budgetary autonomy vis-à-vis the ESC, thus departing from Protocol 16 annexed to the Maastricht Treaty (p. 7).

When presenting his Committee's proposals for the IGC to the EP, *Jacques Blanc*, President of the Committee of the Regions, strongly supported the ideas of an extension in the EP of the obligation to consult the Committee and of a reference in the new Treaty to town and country planning and cross-border collaboration[59]). The CoR wants to fully participate in the IGC and explains in the introduction to its Opinion that this would only be a starting point for further considerations.

f) The Economic and Social Committee

The ESC's report 'The 1996 Intergovernmental Conference: The Role of the Economic and Social Committee', was drawn up by an Ad Hoc Group set up by the Committee Bureau. It was adopted by the Bureau at its meeting on 26 April 1995[60]) and by the plenary on 5 May 1995[61]). The Ad Hoc Group's rapporteur was *G. Cassina*[62]). As the report's title indicates, it deals mainly with the role of the ESC and makes some very detailed proposals for improvements in this respect. In fact, the ESC's report is the only one which actually steps down to the level of concrete formulas for amendments of specific Treaty provisions (see below). However, in its first part it also puts forward general considerations for the future of Europe, especially on the question of what kind of Europe it envisages. Similar to the other institutions, but with a slightly different emphasis, the ESC detects "two major challenges" facing the IGC:

> "to ensure grass-roots involvement in the integration process and to lay the foundations for giving the EU a continental dimension. In other words, the 1996 IGC ought to be paving the way for deepening to coincide with enlargement. Simply consolidating Maastricht

---

[59]) See Agence Europe, 22 June 1995, 4.

[60]) CES 273/95 fin from 4 May 1995.

[61]) According to Agence Europe, 6 May 1995, 4.

[62]) The other members included the ESC President, two Vice-Presidents, the Presidents of the three Groups as co-rapporteurs, and the President of the Section for Economic, Financial and Monetary Questions.

will not tackle these challenges. Fundamental changes must be made (...)." (pt. I.2)

Thus the ESC has stressed on several occasions the 'citizen factor': the "content of deepening (...) must be comprehensible and acceptable to citizens" (pt. I.3); "the proximity of decisions to the citizens (...) should have substance in terms of opportunities and machinery for involvement" (pt. I.3.1); a "democratic and participatory society" should be developed (pt. I.3.2); and the "definition of a legal framework establishing genuine EU citizenship, capable of answering European citizens' needs for identity and democratic participation" should be one of the major aims of the IGC (pt. I.5.8)[63]).

Still on a general level, the ESC calls for an extension of the co-decision procedure; for introducing procedures which underpin the Commission's democratic legitimacy; for democratisation of the process of EMU; for abolishing opt-outs and extending qualified majority voting in social matters; for democratic checks in JHA; and finally for a unitary decision-making framework in order to achieve consistency between commercial policy, development policy, and CFSP (pt. I.5).

When it comes to more specific amendments to the TEU in part II of the report, the ESC concentrates on its own role[64]). In a nutshell, the Committee wants to be involved in more legislative processes than currently, but still act as an advisory body. It asks for its position to be strengthened first by granting it de jure institutional status instead of that of an auxiliary body — one consequence of this being the right to bring an action before the ECJ according to Article 175 (1) ECT (pt. II.11); Second, the ESC calls for the right to send an observer to the deliberations in the Conciliation Committee within co-decision (pt. II.2); Third, it wants legal certainty to be consulted on EU cultural policy (pt. II.5); on the issues of Citizens' Europe (pt. II.4); on association agreements (pt. II.7); and on the use of Article 235 ECT (pt. II.9); Fourth, the Committee asks for recognition of a right to be informed under the procedures

---

[63]) In this context ,it might be useful to provide a reminder of an earlier ESC opinion on 'More Democracy for Europe and Its Institutions; Improved Information for Citizens and Social Actors; the Role of the Ombudsman at the European Parliament', CES(93) 1016 from 21 October 1993, which includes — not yet with specific reference to the forthcoming IGC — some interesting considerations on the future of democracy in the Union.

[64]) We report here in more detail than in other summaries of the contributions to the IGC in part II.A. because no other report deals with the future of the ESC; correspondingly, we did not open a specific ESC title in the key issues' section of this study.

for multilateral surveillance of the economic policies of the Member states (pt. II.3) and on policies in the JHA area (pt. II.8); and finally, concerning its organisational standing, it asks for alignment of its term of office with that of the Commission and the EP, and for the abolition of the Council's and Commission's role in convening the ESC (pt. II.10).

2. Other Prominent Proposals

While the European Council explicitly invited the EC institutions to contribute to the institutional reform debate by preparing reports to the IGC Reflection Group, several independent groups consisting of (mainly) academics and some individual experts have prepared proposals on their own initiative. We will give an overview of the most elaborate and prominent of them below, while further input by many more contributors are included under the relevant specific issues dealt with in later chapters.

a) European Constitutional Group

At the end of 1993, the European Constitutional Group presented to the public its draft for a European Constitution[65]. This group consists of thirteen members from France, Switzerland, Germany, Austria, Italy, Sweden, Spain, and the UK, who are mostly university scholars and often economists[66]. It was formed in summer 1992 "in the belief that the 1996 Intergovernmental Conference should aim to put in place a coherent constitution for Europe" (1a, p. 1).

Its main task was to "provide an alternative agenda to the many centralising proposals that have been made in the past and to put forward instead a positive view of the path of constitutional development in Europe that will lead towards a European Union based in individual freedom" (ibid.). Furthermore, "in order to ensure Europe's future well-being, the Group's proposals stress the importance of clarifying market principles in the constitution" (1a, p. 5). The group 's political option is made explicit with the proposal for asymmetrical decision-rules so that it be "easier to remove market impediments than to impose them" (2b, p. 5). Thus, only simple majorities are suggested "to remove barriers and

---

[65] 'A Proposal for a European Constitution', Report by the European Constitutional Group, December 1993.

[66] They are: *Peter Bernholz, Francisco Cabrillo, Gert Dahlmanns, Jacques Garello, Christian Kirchner, Henri Lepage, Angelo M. Petroni, Joachim Rückert, Pascal Salin, Friedrich Schneider, Peter Stein, Roland Vaubel,* and *Frank Vibert.*

regulations" (2b, p. 6), while a "High Qualified Majority" (4/5 majority) would be necessary to adopt measures "for example in the areas of the environment, health and safety and consumer protection" that "increase regulation or add to costs in the internal market or impede market access for foreign suppliers" (2a, p. 5).

Central features of the proposed European constitution are a catalogue of competencies and strict procedures which generally favour the national level for any such transfers to the supranational level: "The revised Treaty must incorporate defences against creeping centralisation within the Union" (2a, p. 8). In contrast, the Maastricht Treaty is said to "suffer from an artificial attempt to view the Union as potentially the 'optimum domain' in all areas of public and international policy in the new Europe" (2a, p. 3).

The European Constitutional Group's suggested institutional system is explicitly designed to provide for "a strong system of checks and balances" (II, p. 2), primarily aiming at control by national actors over supranational activities. Thus, the Commission is deprived of most of its present powers in the decision-making process. The Council and the two parliamentary chambers (the second one consisting of delegated national parliamentarians) would possess a fully-fledged right of initiative and all three would have to give their assent to any Euro-legislation. The importance of the national levels would also be underlined by a "Union Court of Review" consisting of representatives of national judiciaries as a 'watchdog' against centralising tendencies in the legal sphere.

b) Europäische Strukturkommission (Weidenfeld et al.)

In 1994, under the title 'Europe '96. Reform Programme for the European Union', the 'Europäische Strukturkommission', under the chairmanship of *Werner Weidenfeld*, published its proposals for the future of the EU[67]. This basically German initiative was carried out within a research project on 'strategies and options for Europe' conducted jointly by the 'Forschungsgruppe Europa' (University Mainz) and the Bertelsmann Stiftung. The authors in-

---

[67]) Original in German: *W. Weidenfeld* (ed.), "Europa '96. Reformprogramm für die Europäische Union. Strategien und Optionen für Europa. Erarbeitet von der Europäischen Strukturkommission", Verlag Bertelsmann Stiftung, Gütersloh 1994.

cluded a series of well-known European studies experts[68]) who worked on the proposal for almost two years. It is claimed that the results combine both far-reaching perspectives and realism: the former concerning mainly the federal[69]) and democratic ends, and the latter primarily the specific proposals for structural development of the Union. The centre-piece of the proposal consists of what is called a transparent and democratic decision-making system for a federal and decentralized Europe. However, the authors assume that the dual character of the Union with supranational as well as intergovernmental features will continue to prevail in the future.

The main problems of the Maastricht-style Union are seen in the lack of acceptance by its citizens, the danger of an over-centralisation due to unnecessary shifts of competencies to the European level, the deficit in legitimacy and efficiency, and the insufficient capacity to act in the foreign policy and defence areas (p. 11). In order to promote transparency and restrict centralisation, a thorough redrafting and unifying of the existing Treaties, and a catalogue of competencies ('Kompetenzkatalog') for the Union with strict criteria are suggested (for details see below in the key issues' section).

c) Ludlow/Ersbøll (CEPS)

At the Brussels-based Centre for European Policy Studies (CEPS) a project on the IGC '96 was launched in November 1994. A first analytical paper entitled 'Towards 1996: The Agenda of the Intergovernmental Conference' was written by director *Peter Ludlow*, in collaboration with *Niels Ersbøll*[70]). The first part of the paper outlines some general principles concerning the IGC ("Why a Conference?" and "The Parameters of the Conference") and discusses in its major part the agenda for 1996. *Ludlow/Ersbøll* distinguish six major

---

[68]) They are *Ernst Benda, Klaus von Beyme, Joachim Bitterlich, Karl Dietrich Bracher, Ulrich Everling, Meinhard Hilf, Josef Janning, Peter Graf Kielsmannsegg, Heinz Laufer, Hermann Lübbe, Werner Maihofer, Gert Nicolaysen, Fritz W. Scharpf,* and *Jérôme Vignon.*

[69]) It should be mentioned, however, that the German expression 'föderale Union' does not have the centralist connotation which is accorded to the English 'federalism'. It rather stands for a multi-tiered system with competencies devised between all levels according to (ideally) systematic and structural considerations.

[70]) The paper is contained in CEPS Special Report N° 6 "Preparing for 1996 and a Larger European Union: Principles and Priorities", Brussels 1995. This report also includes the opening address to the CEPS International Advisory Council Conference on 17/18 November 1994 by *Raymond Barre* as well as the programme and the proceedings of the meeting.

subjects: the tasks of the Union; citizenship and rights; institutions; form and presentation; opting in and out; and finally, ratification and entry into force.

Ludlow/Ersbøll agree in principle with the idea of a *Kompetenzkatalog* as launched by the Europäische Strukturkommission, but call for more flexibility (p. 15). They ask that the question of accountability, especially in the second and third pillars, be seriously addressed (p. 28 and 32 f). In the context of citizenship *Ludlow/Ersbøll* give a reminder of the EP's draft text submitted to the Maastricht IGC concerning the principle of non-discrimination in terms of racial, religious, cultural, linguistic, social or national differences (p. 34). With a view to further enlargement and the attachment to the 'principles of democracy' as a criterion of membership (Article F TEU), the paper addresses the possibility that, as a result of regime change, a Member state might start to breach these principles (p. 35). *Ludlow/Ersbøll* go on to suggest more proposals concerning the institutions: they want to see the General Affairs Council become a "clearing house Council" composed of deputy prime ministers who should have a co-ordination function within the national governments (p. 37 f); they call for institutionalisation of the office of the Presidency, and propose to confer on the EP the possibility of a vote of no confidence in the Presidency (p. 39). They are in favour of 'team presidencies' (p. 40) and of a population criterion in qualified majority voting (p. 41). The report is fiercely opposed to any 'Europe à la carte' or 'hard core' model (p. 56 f).

Altogether the report is a preliminary description of the IGC's agenda and contains only punctual and not very elaborate proposals. However, some issues are discussed in a more detailed way, for example the question of how to present the outcome of the next IGC (p. 53 ff.).

d) 'Charlemagne'

A group of anonymous members of the cabinet of the former Secretary-General of the Council of Ministers, and now the Danish representative to the Reflection Group, *Niels Ersbøll*, recently published an article entitled 'L'équilibre entre les États members'[71]) under the pseudonym of 'Charlemagne'. Based on the assumption that the principles of equality among, and liberty of, the Member states could serve as ideal points of references, the text discusses what are called two main problems with a view to a Union of 28

---

[71]) In: Volume in honour of *Niels Ersbøll*, October 1994, pp. 56-80; the text is in French.

Member states: First, the necessary institutional reforms, and second, the question of how to deal with the diversity/heterogeneity in terms of socio-economic factors and political conception of integration.

Under the first heading, *'Charlemagne'* addresses the question of the future scope of the unanimity principle (p. 59 ff.) and acknowledges that it will clearly continue for constitutional questions, with the exception of some nominations such as the one of the Commission's President, for CFSP and certain aspects of JHA. The paper expresses some doubts about the prospects of majority voting within social policy and fiscal decisions, and concludes that "it seems today that the field of application of qualified majority has reached its limits" (p. 62, our translation). They see a "noyau dur", a hard core of policies where majority voting could only be introduced with prudence. *'Charlemagne'* goes on to discuss the weighting of votes in cases of qualified majority voting and argues that mechanic extrapolation of the present system to a Union of 28 members would lead to unacceptable consequences: first, a minority of 47 % of the European population could, in principle, constitute a qualified majority and, second, the smaller states of Eastern and Central Europe acting as a group could form a blocking minority (p. 65). The paper proposes a re-weighting of the votes in order to reduce the disproportion which so far favours the small countries, and recommends some guiding principles in that respect (p. 66).

The second major part of *'Charlemagne's'* contribution is devoted to the problem of different tracks of integration which will be even more important in an enlarged Union (p. 68 ff.). The model of 'variable geometry' is advocated (see III.B.1.b1). The paper argues, however, that the concept has some important limits and political and legal difficulties, which could only be overcome if some precautions were taken (p. 76 f).

e) *'Justus Lipsius'*

In an article titled 'The 1996 Intergovernmental Conference', an "international civil servant" [obviously from the EC Council[72)] under the pseudonym 'Justus Lipsius' reflects on goals and options for the IGC 1996[73]). The two major challenges are seen in the enlargement from 15 to 26 states (the

---

[72]) According to *Miller* (1995, note 19), Lipsius "is widely reputed to be a senior official in the Council secretariat".

[73]) Published in European Law Journal 3/1995 (pages cited from manuscript); a French version of the text appeared in the Revue Trimestrielle de Droit européen 2/1995.

11 additional ones being the six Central and Eastern European Countries, the three Baltic States, Cyprus and Malta) and in gaining the "full and whole-hearted support of the citizens of the Union" (p. 1). In order to meet those challenges, *'Lipsius'* thinks that the negotiators will have to "inject in the Union more flexibility, more efficiency, more consistency, more democracy, more subsidiarity and more clarity" (p. 1).

Concerning the suggested solution for institutional problems and challenges, *'Lipsius'* mostly refers to already debated models while giving his views on the pros and cons. Often he suggests a preferred solution and then goes on to describe second best solutions if the first one should be "politically inopportune". Clearly, the Council is in the centre of his thinking of the EC system. Compared to most other authors, he is more reluctant to admit the existence of a democratic deficit. However, he sees "possible ways of improving the democratic legitimacy of the decision-making process in the EU" (p. 35) and suggests simultaneously enhancing the EP's powers; giving a greater role to national parliaments; and improving the democratic representativeness of the votes in the Council.

f) Federal Trust Round Table

The Federal Trust for Education and Research[74] has established a Round Table[75] to discuss the issues raised by the IGC '96; to monitor the processes of its preparation, negotiation and ratification; and to assess its outcome. From February 1995 onwards it published a series of 'Federal Trust Papers': the first contains general remarks on the 'State of the Union' and the prospects of the IGC '96, the second remarks on EMU, and the third some detailed proposals on institutional reform[76]).

---

[74]) FT is a non-governmental London-based organisation founded in 1945 and devoted to the study of "the future of democratic unity between states and peoples" with a principal focus on the European Union and the U.K.'s role within it. The Chairman of FT is *John Pinder*, the Director *Andrew Duff*.

[75]) FT Paper N° 3 lists 84 members of the Round Table, among them well-known scholars, public servants, MPs and MEPs; to name just a few of them: *Lord Lenkins of Hillhead* (chair), *J. Pinder* (rapporteur), *A. Duff* (secretary), *H. and W. Wallace, S. Strange, V. Bogdanor, W. Wessels, A. Butt Philip, R. Corbett, F. Jacobs, D. Martin, M. Shackleton, J.-V. Louis, A. Marr, S. Williams*, etc.

[76]) 'Building the Union: Reform of the Union. The Intergovernmental Conference of the European Union 1996', Federal Trust Papers N° 3, June 1995. According to footnote 1, the

The Round Table opposes further extension of the Union's competencies but suggests a series of reforms to improve the institutional set-up: the main proposals are strengthening the protection of fundamental rights and freedoms; opening the legislative sessions of the Council to press and public; improving accountability of ministers to home parliaments; requiring all laws to be approved by the EP as well as by the Council; tightening the control of agricultural spending by giving the Parliament equal powers with the Council, as for other budgetary expenditure; cutting the number of Commissioners to a maximum of one from each Member state; strengthening the powers to check fraud and lax financial control by Member states in spending Union money and to punish those responsible; and extending the jurisdiction of the ECJ so that citizens may have recourse to judicial remedies with respect to any action by the Union's institutions.

The paper of the mainly British Round Table also addresses the problem of variable geometry and the relationship between a core group of Member states prepared to deepen integration and others which are not going to participate in these efforts. In contrast to the stance of the British government, however, the Round Table strongly advocates that Britain join a possible core group.

g) The Herman Report

The tradition of presenting far-reaching constitutional proposals is important in the European Parliament. Most prominently, it presented on 14 February 1984 its well-known Draft Proposal for a European Union, the so-called Spinelli initiative[77]). With a view to the IGC 1996, a 'Project of a Working Document on the Constitution of the European Union'[78]) was presented on 1 April 1993 by the then rapporteur, *M. Oreja Aguirre,* on behalf of the Institutional Committee. This was followed by a first [15 September 1993[79])] and

---

main contributor to this paper was John Pinder, assisted by a working party composed of members of the Round Table under the chairmanship of *David Martin*, MEP. The proposal for the uniform electoral procedure of the EP has been drafted by *Karel De Gucht* and *Andrew Duff.*

[77]) OJ 84/C 77/33.

[78]) PE 203.601/rev. 1.

[79]) PE 203.601/B.

second 'Report on a Constitution of the European Union' (27 January 1994)[80]) by rapporteur *F. Herman* as the successor of Mr. *Oreja Aguirre*. The report was accepted by the Committee but resubmitted to it by the plenary on 9 February 1994. The final version was then adopted by the EP on 10 February 1994. Nevertheless, the Parliament decided not to continue work on the document until the new EP was elected on 12 June 1994. So far, the new MEPs have not resumed the work on the draft Constitution, but only elaborated a report on the functioning of the TEU which rather follows a step-by-step approach (see above III.A.1.b).

The Herman Report outlines in depth the reasons for the EP launching a new discussion on a European constitution, carefully distinguishing between political, legal and ethical grounds (B.II and III). It suggests a "federal model with co-operative and decentralised structure" as opposed to a "confederational", a "federal", and a "federal model on the basis of regions" (B.IV). The report includes a comprehensive and detailed draft constitution which was submitted to the other institutions, the governments, and national parliaments for further discussion (pt. 6 of EP's Resolution 10.2.94). The EP furthermore proposed that a European constitutional convention, with delegates from the European and the national parliaments, be convened before the 1996 IGC (pt. 2), and that another inter-institutional conference be held (pt. 4).

The proposed constitution of the European Union consists of VIII Titles and only 47 Articles. In contrast to the 1984 Draft Treaty it is not designed to entirely replace the constitutional framework as it stands at the moment, i.e. the seventeen Treaties or other acts of same value. The present Treaties (the ECT, the Maastricht Treaty, etc.) would remain in force in so far as they do not contradict the Constitution (Article 8); as the Constitution would not contain any specific list of competencies of activities of the Union all these provisions could remain applicable. Therefore, the proposed constitution has "another legal value [than the other Treaties][81]) and creates a stable and permanent framework" (B.V). The bulk of provisions concern the institutional framework, a new hierarchy of laws, the decision-making procedure and a list of human and fundamental rights. Only a few of these new rules differ considerably from the present system, but most of them fit well in our list of key issues for the IGC. Therefore, it seems reasonable to discuss the details of the proposed Con-

---

[80]) PE 203.601/endg.2 - A3-0064/94.

[81]) Our interpretation.

stitution in the next part of the study, together with the other proposals for 1996. However, one should bear in mind that the Constitution as proposed by rapporteur Herman and endorsed by the Institutional Committee, as well as the plenary of the former EP symbolises much more than the sum of its detailed Articles can indicate.

3. Prominent Political Contributions from Single Member States

Under this heading, we shall present a number of prominent proposals by national political actors concerning the future political system of the European Union[82]) — all dating from within a few months before the formal preparation of the IGC began at the level of high diplomats in summer 1995. These outlines represent mostly snap-shots of the governments' thoughts (or of senior members or parties thereof) before any official national position was adopted. Clearly thus, the national options are themselves still somewhat in flux, and may well be adapted later on to the political surrounding within the intergovernmental bargaining. One must also take into consideration that the composition of some governments might change before the final showdown of the IGC. Be this as it may, for any more elaborate and official input to the IGC (not to mention its results) we shall have to wait for many more months. Thus, the early signs outlined underneath are of immense interest in order to get a first glance of what lowest common denominators, on the one hand, and possible subjects for package deals, on the other, might look like.

a) Belgian Positions

Speaking to the College of Europe in Natolin (Poland) as Belgian *Prime Minister, Jean-Luc Dehaene* set out his intentions for the IGC 1996. Not surprisingly (as his country has traditionally been at the forefront of European integration), he argued that according to the Belgian experience, "formally abandoning sovereignty to the European Union might often result in a considerable increase of real influence exerted"[83]). While open for any debate on details within institutional reform, he stressed that Belgium very much appreciated

---

[82]) Many more statements by national politicians on single issues (including from Member states not included at this stage) are mentioned in the outline of the main issues to be negotiated during the IGC, below. To find out about relevant contributions under this heading we mainly relied on the reports of the prominent European news service, Agence Europe.

[83]) Cited from Agence Europe, 20 January 1995, 3.

"the institutional equilibrium between the Council, the Commission, Parliament and the Court of Justice" (ibid.). Concerning the increased divergence in an ever larger Union, some kind of differentiation might be useful — a 'Europe à la carte', however, was nothing Belgium could favour (ibid.).

The very European-minded stance of Belgium was also proven by the advisory committee on European affairs of the *Belgian parliament*, which is composed of members of the Belgian House of Representatives and the EP. It affirmed in an interim report on the IGC that Belgium "must refuse all enlargement of the Union unless the Conference results in credible deepening"[84]). Therefore, the rule of unanimity should be given up as far as possible, even in the second and third pillars.

b) Germany: CDU/CSU Paper

On 1 September 1994, two leading politicians of the major fraction in the German Bundestag (christian-democrat CDU/CSU), *Wolfgang Schäuble* and *Karl Lamers*, presented a paper entitled 'Reflections on European Policy'[85]). The paper addresses the idea of a European Constitution (a "constitution-like document") with a fixed list of competencies for the EU, the Member states, and the regions, based on federal principles and subsidiarity.

With respect to institutional developments, the CDU/CSU paper proposes reforms and the "re-weighting of all institutions": it suggests that the Council become a second, i.e. a states' chamber, and the Commission a European government; and it stresses the crucial role of national parliaments in European politics (p. 5). Furthermore it contains a series of contentious reflections on the future of the CFSP, NATO and WEU.

What the document became known for is its discussion of increased differentiation in European integration with clear emphasis on a strong centre. Starting from their assumption that the "institutional development has to combine cohesion and consistency with elasticity and flexibility" (p. 6, our translation), *Schäuble/Lamers* fiercely oppose the 'Europe à la carte' model and call

---

[84]) Quoted from Agence Europe, 10 April 1995, 2.

[85]) CDU/CSU-Fraktion des Deutschen Bundestages, 'Überlegungen zur europäischen Politik', Bonn 1. 9. 1994, N° 10793; an English version has been published in *Lamers*, 'A German Agenda for the European Union', Federal Trust and Konrad Adenauer Stiftung, London 1994; we cite here from the German original (our translations); see also Agence Europe, 27 August 1993, 2.

for realisation of the models of 'variable geometry' *or* 'different speeds', despite all legal and practical difficulties: "It is decisive that those countries which are willing and able to go further in their co-operation and in the integration process should not be blocked by veto rights of other members" (p. 6, our translation). This group of some five to six Member states would form the so-called 'hard core' ('fester Kern') with an 'inner core' ('Kern des festen Kerns'), i.e. France and Germany[86]).

Although the CDU/CSU is at present the governing party, this paper does not represent an official statement by the German government. Several press statements revealed that the suggestions had not been thoroughly co-ordinated with either the Federal Ministry of Foreign Affairs or with all relevant parts of the two parties, but that in fact it had a strong personal imprint of the two main authors *Karl Lamers* and *Wolfgang Schäuble*. Chancellor *Kohl*'s spokesperson said that these thoughts were not yet government policy, but "there is no question of distancing ourselves from them"[87]). Be that as it may, the paper considerably influenced the debates which followed[88]). Commentators also detected similarities with the content of *Balladur*'s interview in Le Figaro[89]).

c) France: Guéna Report

It is beyond doubt that France is the Member state where the debate on the 1996 IGC started earliest, and has been the most vivid so far. Within the institutional field, it is mainly the idea of introducing a second parliamentary chamber with national parliamentarians that has had much response — if mostly critical.

On 19 February 1995, Senator *Yves Guéna* presented his report 'On the 1996 Reform of the Institutions of the European Union', on behalf of the delegation of the French Senate for the European Union[90]). This text is not in-

---

[86]) For these notions see below III.B.1.b.1.

[87]) Cited from Agence Europe, 5/6 September 1994, 2.

[88]) See e.g. Agence Europe, 5/6 September 1994, 2; 7 September 1994, 3; 14 September 1994, 3 f, 5 November 1994, 5.

[89]) See point d) below.

[90]) Rapport d'information n° 224, deuxième session extraordinaire 1994-1995, sur 'la réforme de 1996 des institutions de l'Union européenne'. The *Senate* is the second parliamentary chamber representing the regional and local level in France (régions, départements, etc); the *Sénateurs* are indirectly elected by regional and local assemblies.

tended "to propose a comprehensive answer to all the problems which will come up in 1996 but rather to voice certain reflections shared by the majority of the Senate" (p. 8, our translation). The report does not advocate any merging of the three pillars and is consequently devised in three parts dealing with each pillar separately. It even proposes new institutions for the second and third pillars, such as two Secretariats-General for CFSP and JHA (p. 44).

Guéna proposes a European Senate (p. 39 f and 45) representing the national parliaments. This body should be given control and advisory functions in the second and third pillars, and the task of controlling the respect of the principle of subsidiarity within the first pillar (p. 14). The report adopted by the French Senate furthermore calls for a system of team Presidencies and a double majority of both votes and population in the Council (p. 17). In order to counterbalance the loss of influence of the smaller countries with respect to the Presidency, *Guéna* proposes the reduction of the number of Commissioners not by taking the right to one Commissioner from the smaller countries, but by taking the right to a second from the larger ones (p. 19). The report furthermore asks the IGC to release an interpretative protocol which aims at defining more precisely (and, indeed, reducing) the legislative competencies of the Commission within the implementation of EC policies (p. 20 f).

The Senate's report makes hardly any proposals aimed at enhancing the European Parliament's powers. In fact, *Guéna* even wants to reduce the range of texts submitted to it (p. 23). In contrast, there is a lot to be found about enhancing the role of national parliaments: in addition to the idea of a European Senate (see above), there are for example some considerations concerning the transmission of the Commission's proposals to them (p. 24) and the participation of representatives of national parliaments in the formation of some Council delegations (p. 25). Furthermore, it is proposed to submit each inter-institutional agreement to a simplified ratification procedure in the national parliaments (p. 24).

d) *France: Interview by the Former Prime Minister, Speech by the Later President*

In August 1994, the then Prime Minister, *Edouard Balladur,* suggested a Europe of three circles in order to meet the contradicting challenges of widening and preserving the Union's cohesion and objectives for integration[91]). The outer circle should be the CSCE, including countries which would for a long time not be members of the Union: "We must build with them a diplomatic and security organisation and form economic and commercial links"[92]). The middle circle would accordingly be the current Union based on the Maastricht Treaty, and the inner one a more structured organisation in the fields of monetary affairs and defence. This matter was, in his eyes, "well underway, at the initiative of France and Germany"[93]). While all Union members should be invited to join, it was highly unlikely that all would be able and wish to do so.

When presenting his ideas on foreign policy and European policy six months later, the now French President, *Jacques Chirac,* advocated a variable geometry: "The Member states that wish to go faster and further together should be able to do so"[94]). Concerning institutional affairs, he underlined the role of the Council of Ministers, which he wants to see strengthened via a right of initiative and a prolonged period of the Presidency. The votes should be adapted to take "political realities" better into account, and a link created between different parameters, including population. Furthermore, he suggested that a President of the Union be elected for a period of three years to represent the Union externally. Like the French Senate suggested one month earlier, he also wants national parliaments to be more closely associated to the Community and involved in the development of Union standards.

e) Ireland: Speech by the Foreign Minister

In his speech on the future of integration on 22 May 1995[95]), the Irish Foreign Minister *Dick Spring* showed a rather conservative stance concerning institutional reforms. He stressed his country's interest in strong central institutions within which small countries' voices would be best heard. Therefore, Ireland wants to keep the right to nominate a Commissioner as well as the unanimity requirement "when very fundamental national concerns are at stake". Ireland does not see a real danger that the larger countries be outvoted in the Council. However, *Spring* wants the status of the EP enhanced through expansion of the

---

[91]) Le Figaro, 30 August 1994.

[92]) Citation from the translation in Agence Europe 3 September 1994, 1.

[93]) Citation from the translation in Agence Europe 3 September 1994, 1.

[94]) Cited from Agence, Europe 23 March 1995, 2.

[95]) See Agence Europe, 24 May 1995, 3 f.

co-decision procedure, while seeking at the same time to enhance the role of the national parliaments.

f) Great Britain: Speech by the Prime Minister

In a much quoted speech at the University of Leiden on 7 September 1994, the British Prime Minister, *John Major*, outlined his view on the reform debate and reacted to the paper of the German CDU/CSU. Accordingly, the British attitude vis-à-vis the challenges facing Europe centres around the importance of the nation state (even when it comes to confer democratic legitimacy on the European polity) as well as the notion of flexibility. The only area where Major seems to be ready to make European rules more binding for all members is the field of implementation of EC law and the fight against fraud (p. 7)[96]). As he outlined on later occasions, *Major* thinks that "the returning of decisions back to the nation state has got widespread support across the European Community"[97]). While asking that national parliaments be involved in EC decision-making, *Major* said he would not accept constitutional change that impacts on the British parliament[98]). That the British will be uneasy partners within the IGC is also proven by the fact that the then employment Secretary, Michael Portillo, openly stated that the UK would, within this conference, have recourse to veto to prevent further progress in European integration[99]).

g) Spain: Government Paper

The Spanish government has presented a report on "The 1996 Conference — Bases for Discussion" which promotes an integrationist attitude on the one hand, and Spanish financial interests on the other. First, the document insists on the need to maintain two fundamental elements which might be endangered by former suggestions of other delegations: the single institutional framework and the preservation of the acquis communautaire. It also "gives ideas that are currently circulating and which would directly or indirectly affect these principles, such as that concerning 'abusive application' of subsidiarity, revision of CAP and structural policy, and strengthening of the Council to the detriment of

---

[96]) See also the statement of the British representative in the reflection group, *Davis*, in Agence Europe 18 February 1995, 4.

[97]) Cited from Agence Europe, 30 January 1995, 4.

[98]) Agence Europe, 9 January 1995, 3.

[99]) See Agence Europe, 30 January 1995, 4.

the other institutions"[100]). While the Spanish would themselves opt for a European constitution, they do not expect the other delegations to follow that path and thus aim at least at a simplification of the Treaties and at inclusion of fundamental rights. Concerning more flexibility within the European architecture, they suggest "as a last resort" to allow for 'variable geometry' based on firm principles (see below). Voting should be reformed so that population be taken into account.

B. The Key Issues

In the following second part of the chapter on the current reform debate, we shall outline the major points at stake related to institutional reform of the European Union and, more generally, the future of democracy at the European level. Within the three chapters: (1.) structure of the Union; (2.) institutional matters; and (3.) procedural matters, the many detailed suggestions discussed in (amongst others) the prominent proposals outlined above will be studied in a series of sub-chapters. We built these sub-categories mainly by analysing and grouping the various contributions to the IGC. At the end of each chapter, we shall sketch out what might be appropriate options from a specific Austrian perspective, bearing in mind this country's constitutional, as well as pragmatic, choices concerning its political system.

1. Structure of the Union

This first range of questions include matters concerning the overall architecture of the European political system: Should it be based on a constitutional charter which possibly guarantees fundamental human (and even social?) rights? Should the present system of three "pillars" with different sets of institutional and competence rules be prolonged? How about more flexibility for differentiated integration within diverse policy fields — possibly at the expense of unity? Shall the principle of subsidiarity be reformulated, and a hierarchy of legislative acts be developed? Should individual Member states be allowed or even forced to step out of the Union? And, last but not least, how could the relationship between the Union and its citizens be improved?

a) Should There Be a European Constitution?

---

[100]) Agence Europe, 11 March 1995, 4.

When considering the simple provision in Article N (2) TEU, calling for a revision of those few provisions which actually provide for their own reassessment in 1996, it seems quite astonishing that on this occasion the question of drafting a European Constitution is again on the political agenda[101]). As outlined in the introduction, a series of developments have widened the scope of the IGC to a point where some argue that the time for a Constitution has come. From the discussion it becomes clear that two lines of reasoning converge at some point: the first being the more fundamental aspiration to solve the pressing problems of the Union with a single stroke (i.), the second being the rather pragmatic perception of the necessity to redraft the Union framework in order to make it more accessible and appealing for the European citizens (ii.).

(i.) For instance, the *FT Round Table* asks the IGC to "lay down a process for converting the Treaty into a constitutional document that makes clear to the citizens what the Union's powers are and how its governance works"[102]). The *CDU/CSU paper* calls for "a constitution-like document (...) delimiting the respective competencies of the EU, the Member states and the regions in clear language and defining the ideal basis of the Union". This document should be oriented towards the federal state model and the principle of subsidiarity[103]). The *Europäische Strukturkommission* does not explicitly ask for a "constitution" to be drawn up. However, it suggests replacing the existing Treaties with a single and simplified text which would clearly be at least the functional equivalent of a constitution[104]). *'Justus Lipsius'* suggests that it would be ideal to replace the existing number of treaties by one "Treaty-Charter" which should be "as short and readable as possible, dealing with principles, competence and institutional matters, and on the other hand, a number of Protocols annexed to it, dealing in detail with specific matters, such as the Internal Market"[105]). The new and single entity, the European Union, should be given legal personality and treaty making power[106]). According to the document on "the elements of a Spanish position" drawn up by the chair of the IGC

---

[101]) Interestingly, the CoR calls the Maastricht Treaty "a European constitutional text", CdR 136/95, 2.

[102]) Federal Trust Papers N° 3, 6.

[103]) CDU/CSU September 1994, 5 (our translation).

[104]) Europäische Strukturkommission 1994, 14 f.

[105]) *'Justus Lipsius'* 1995, 52.

[106]) *'Justus Lipsius'* 1995, 51.

reflection group, *Carlos Westendorp*, the Conference should lead to the adoption of a fundamental text of quasi-constitutional nature, which is clear and understandable to the public[107]). This Spanish preference was repeated in a later text "The 1996 Conference — Bases for Discussion" presented by the Foreign Minister, *Javier Solana*, to the Spanish Parliament. Again, the advantages of a Constitution, i.e. transparency, clarity, comprehensibility for citizens, were underlined[108]).

The *CoR* is the only EU organ at the moment which explicitly calls for a "basic text" which should include provisions concerning the fundamental rights of the European citizens, the aims of the European Union, the institutions of the Union, and the competencies of these institutions[109]).

Apart from several proposals dating from before the Maastricht Treaty[110]), there are also two recent and widely discussed examples for the 'qualitative leap' policy: First, the *European Constitutional Group* has already with its choice of name expressed its thorough belief in the need for a constitution. A respective text is suggested[111]). Obviously, the Group's picture of the future of European integration digresses considerably, not only from the present institutional structure but also from underlying guiding principles in European policy, such as establishing a social market economy rather than, as they suggest, a radically liberal regime. Therefore, the reason for drafting a completely new constitutional framework clearly lays in the simple necessity to change almost everything and thus in the impossibility to build on the acquis communautaire.

Second, the *Herman Report,* too, is not only clearly in favour of a European Constitution but also proposes an elaborated draft. Herman argues that the existing Treaties together with some other acts of equal value, some leading principles drawn from the jurisprudence of the ECJ (direct applicability and primacy), and a series of special rights conferred upon the citizens of the Union, *already* constitute a constitutional legal order. Furthermore, the Treaties

---

[107]) See Agence Europe, 11 February 1995, 3.

[108]) However, the document also underlines the "powerful nationalistic reflexes" which would no doubt prevent it, and states that whatever the form chosen, a simplification of the existing Treaties be necessary (Agence Europe, 11 March 1995, 4).

[109]) CoR Resolution from 20 April 1995, CdR 136/95, pt. 14.

[110]) E.g. Parliament's Draft Treaty on European Union 1984, or the proposals by *Allais* 1991.

[111]) European Constitutional Group 1993.

also contain a lot of provisions without constitutional status[112]). Thus, his first call is for simplification and transparency. However, this could also be realised in another, better written treaty. The argument pro constitution then is two-fold. First, he describes European integration as being based on the theory of double legitimacy: via the citizens represented in the European Parliament, and via the Member states represented in the Council. The principle of democracy would not be fully satisfied where a treaty is signed only by the states. In contrast, a constitution would *also* be formulated and decided by the EP, and therefore higher ranking in terms of democracy[113]). Second, a constitution would put an end to the fiction of still untouched sovereignty of the Member states and of the ambiguity allowing the national governments to blame Brussels for failures and to attribute success to themselves[114]). The proposed Constitution of the *Herman Report* should enter into force if the majority of Member states representing at least four fifths of the population ratified it. Those Member states which could not ratify in due time would either have to withdraw or stay in the changed Union. In case of withdrawal special agreements between the Union and these Member states should treat them as privileged associated partners similar to the status in the EEA agreement[115]).

Clearly, the whole idea of a formal constitution calls for strong reactions of both the "anti-federalists" and the "federalists". To cite just a few examples, *John Major*, on the one hand, stated that he believed "that the Nation State will remain the basic political unit in Europe"[116]). *Major* said he would not accept constitutional change that impacts on the British parliament[117]), and: "I am as passionately opposed to a wholly federal Europe as I would be to Britain losing its membership of the European Union"[118]). On the other hand, according to information on a recent opinion poll by the *Italian* European Federalist Movement, "88 % of voters were in favour of attributing a constituent mandate in

---

[112]) Herman Report 1994, II.2 and III.B.1.

[113]) Herman Report 1994, III.C.2.

[114]) Herman Report 1994, II.3.

[115]) Herman Report 1994, Article 47 of the proposed Constitution.

[116]) *John Major*, Speech at the University of Leiden, 7 September 1994, p. 5 of manuscript.

[117]) *Major* cited from Agence Europe, 9 January 1995, 3.

[118]) Cited from Agence Europe, 23 December 1994, 1.

the European Parliament"[119]). And during a symposium in March 1995 organised by the PDS and the Socialist Group in the *EP*, a federation of States in Europe was suggested[120]).

(ii.) Obviously, consensus on a radical departure — i.e. putting in place a fully-fledged European Constitution with all the political symbolism involved in national constitutions[121]) — is very unlikely at the moment. But there is still another, much more pragmatic aspect of this debate: consolidating the Treaties in order to enhance the comprehensibility of the Union's framework, along with rewording and amending the parts on European citizenship, could be a way of constitutionalising the Union. Even the *Commission* argues "that the Union's basic treaties are difficult to read and understand, which is hardly likely to mobilise public opinion in their favour"[122]). It considers that the "three Communities and the Union should be merged into a single entity, as should the Treaties (...)"[123]). Furthermore, the Commission's report advocates a "fundamental text" listing the rights and duties of the European citizens[124]). A similar route is also suggested by the EP resolution: the Treaty should be rewritten in order to simplify and make it more appealing to the citizens; for example the provisions concerning citizens' rights should be placed at the beginning, those covering the institutions and those covering the content of policies should be separated and out-of-date articles deleted[125]). One specific proposal made in the *EP*'s IGC resolution is to bring together within a single article the economic rights that are scattered throughout the Treaty (such as the right to free movement and establishment of labour and of the professions), and to reinforce these rights[126]). The *ECJ* also favours a codification and settlement of the primary law[127]).

---

[119]) Agence Europe, 6 March 1995, 5.

[120]) Agence Europe, 6 March 1995, 5.

[121]) As *Ludlow/Ersbøll* (CEPS) 1995, 54, put it: a constitution should "capture the higher ground".

[122]) Commission Report, SEC(95) 731, 34.

[123]) Commission Report, SEC(95) 731, 34.

[124]) Commission Report, SEC(95) 731, 4.

[125]) EP Resolution from 17. 5. 1995, PE 190.441, pt. 2.

[126]) EP Resolution from 17. 5. 1995, PE 190.441, pt. 7.

[127]) ECJ Report from May 1995, pt. 23.

Ludlow/Ersbøll argue that "the form and even the tone in which the inter-governmental agreement is presented to the public will be crucial for its immediate acceptability and its long term durability. The final text must be clear and appealing."[128]) They highlight three considerations as regards this all but easy task: the European voters ought to be made aware of the values for which Europe stands and of the obligations as well as the rights that membership of the Union entails; the Treaty should be consolidated and simplified; and finally, they propose that the European Council commission an "official introduction and commentary written in non-technical language"[129]).

(1) The Protection of Fundamental Rights in the EU

One important aspect of constitutionalising the European Union is the question of how to deal with the protection of fundamental rights. This is a long-standing debate which led to considerable tension between some national constitutional courts and the ECJ over the question if there is appropriate protection of the basic rights by the ECJ (which is closely related to the doctrine of supremacy of EU law even over constitutional law of the Member states). The ECJ's position which has been accepted over the years by the national courts is based on the acknowledgement that the fundamental rights be an unwritten part of the Community's primary law. The Court protects them as part of the general principles of Community law against violation by secondary Community legislation. The Court draws on the Convention on the Protection of Human Rights and Fundamental Freedoms of the Council of Europe (CoE) and on the national provisions. Article F (2) TEU took this established practice on board. Without going into the details of this difficult area, one can conclude that although the Community practice respects the fundamental rights, their protection in the Union context might nevertheless be improved. Therefore, a change of the situation is under discussion. Apart from the *FT Round Table*'s proposal to simply insert in the Treaty a provision explicitly charging the Court with the task of ensuring that the institutions respect the fundamental rights[130]), there are two major alternatives:

First, the Union (or the European Community) could join the European Convention. Whether this is at least legally possible for the Union/Community,

---

[128]) *Ludlow/Ersbøll* (CEPS) 1995, 53.

[129]) *Ludlow/Ersbøll* (CEPS) 1995, 55.

[130]) Federal Trust Papers N° 3, 26 f.

is currently the subject of a pending request for an opinion before the ECJ. Among others the *EP*[131]) and the *Federal Trust Round Table*[132]) favour this alternative.

The other option would be for the EU to draw up a catalogue of fundamental rights as part of the primary law of the Union, i.e. as a part of the TEU or a formal European Constitution.

The *Europäische Strukturkommission* thinks that generally, a democratic community ought to have basic rights established and enshrined in a treaty by the directly legitimised institutions (for the Union they seem to suggest that this be both the EP and the national parliaments). Only this could give any judicial system the necessary amount of authority, democratic basis and acceptance[133]).

The *German Bundesrat* requested that the possibility of introducing a list of fundamental rights in the Treaty be examined[134]). The chair of the IGC reflection group, Carlos Westendorp, asked in a document on "the elements of a *Spanish* position" for the adoption of a Charter on Fundamental Rights and Liberties which would be protected by the Court of Justice in Luxembourg[135]). In a government paper, the chapter on Union citizenship of the Maastricht Treaty is called one "to which Spain made a decisive contribution" and which should be considerably extended concerning the rights included[136]). The *CoR* asked that the revision of the Treaty give rise to the "drawing up of a founding text" and that a catalogue of fundamental rights be included[137]). The Committee of the Regions wants to be involved more explicitly in action in these areas[138]).

As to the *content* of such a list, a series of proposals have been made, with the Europäische Strukturkommission and the Herman Report's being the most

---

[131]) EP Resolution from 17. 5. 1995, PE 190.441, pt. 7.

[132]) Federal Trust Papers N° 3, 6.

[133]) Europäische Strukturkommission 1994, 42.

[134]) Agence Europe, 1 April 1995, 3.

[135]) See Agence Europe, 11 February 1995, 3.

[136]) Agence Europe, 11 March 1995, 6.

[137]) See Pujol report, cited from AE 24. 4. 1995, 4.

[138]) In addition, to consider that in the case of having a fundamental rights catalogue in the Treaty, Article 173 (5) ECT might not be enough to ensure effective protection of fundamental rights in the framework of legislative activity by the Union institutions: ECJ Report from May 1995, pt. 20.

elaborated ones: The *Europäische Strukturkommission* suggests a limitation to the "essential basic and human rights", including dignity, the equality principle, the respect for ones physical integrity, and freedom of the individual, as well as derogated rights such as right to property and professional freedom. While the inclusion of detailed social rights is left open for political negotiation within the Member states, the Strukturkommission considers at least basic social rights to be necessary within the Internal Market[139]). The Constitution proposed by the *Herman Report* includes in its Title VIII a list of "Human Rights Guaranteed by the Union". The lists has 24 items, ranging from the right to life, the freedom of thought, including the right to conscientious objection, the protection of the family, to some social rights (such as the right to work) and collective social rights (including the freedom to strike). The ECJ would be responsible for actions by individuals claiming violation of these human rights by the Union[140]). The current *Parliament* urges in its resolution for the "inclusion of an explicit reference in the Treaty to the principle of equal treatment irrespective of race, sex, age, handicap or religion (including mentioning the fundamental social rights of workers set out in the Charter[141]), enlarging upon them and extending them to all citizens of the Union)"; a ban on capital punishment; the application of the provisions in the Treaty on equal rights not only to economic rights but to all aspects of equality for women[142]).

"The elements of a *Spanish* position" requested for the inclusion of a specific article on xenophobia and racism[143]). *Parliament* makes a similar proposal by asking for

> "a clear rejection [in the Treaty] of racism, xenophobia, sexism, discrimination on grounds of a person's sexual orientation, anti-Semitism, revisionism and all forms of discrimination and guarantee adequate legal protection against discrimination for all individuals resident within the EU."[144])

---

[139]) Europäische Strukturkommission 1994, 42.

[140]) Herman Report 1994, Article 38 of the proposed Constitution.

[141]) I.e. the so-called Social Charter (text published e.g. by the Office for Official Publications of the EC, 1990).

[142]) EP Resolution from 17. 5. 1995, PE 190.441, pt. 7.

[143]) Agence Europe, 11 March 1995, 6.

[144]) EP Resolution from 17. 5. 1995, PE 190.441, pt. 7.

(2) The Future of the Three-Pillar System

While adding a third pillar to the Union (the second had already been introduced by the SEA), the Maastricht Treaty nevertheless calls for a re-assessment of the pillar structure[145]). Justice and home affairs (JHA) were left outside the ordinary Community framework, which means that not only different and far less democratic decision-making rules are applicable, but also that the ECJ is not competent in this sector — which is of great importance for the individual. Furthermore, the present three-pillar structure has anything but increased transparency of the Union framework.

We can distinguish two different solutions to these problems: either to merge the pillars (at least the third into the first pillar) (i.), or to improve at least their structure (ii.):

(i.) On the one hand, the *Commission* concluded its assessment of "the institutional response to the requirement for legitimacy" with an overall positive answer but makes a reservation concerning "the weakness, not to say the absence, of democratic control at Union level in the fields of activity where the intergovernmental process still holds away."[146]) In its conclusions the Commission speaks about "the less-than-convincing experience with intergovernmental co-operation under the second and third pillars" and recommends it inadvisable to seek further enlargement on this basis. Against the Background of its conclusions on the necessity of majority voting and participation of the Parliament, the *FT Round Table* considers the transfer of the third pillar into Community competence as the simplest and best solution[147]). By definition, the three-pillar-system would disappear with the proposed Constitution in the *Herman Report*[148]). The *ESC* wants to give "the Community responsibility for justice and home-affairs policies", arguing that "these issues are too important and too sensitive for European citizens to be confined to the intergovernmental sphere without democratic checks, at the risk, inter alia, of creating two speeds and discrimination"[149]). With respect to the first pillar, the ESC points at the necessity to achieve consistency between commercial policy, development co-op-

---

145) See Article B dash 5 TEU.

146) Commission Report, SEC(95) 731, 18.

147) Federal Trust Papers N° 3, 31.

148) See Herman Report 1994, Articles 41 ff. of the proposed Constitution.

149) CES 273/95 fin, pt. I.5.9.

eration policy, and CFSP, and consequently calls for a unitary decision-making framework[150]). Taken together, these two demands add up to a total merging of the three pillars.

On the other hand, the *Guéna Report* is strongly opposed to a merger of the second and third pillars into the first: "In these sectors specific modes of co-operation and decision-making are necessary."[151]) Their character of intergov-ernmentalism should be rather reinforced and new efficient institutions set up, such as two Secretariats-General for each of the pillars and a European Senate of representatives of the national parliaments[152]). Also for pragmatic reasons, the *Europäische Strukturkommission* thinks that the IGC 1996 will more than likely not be able to end the specific, and rather intergovernmental, features of European co-operation in the fields of internal and justice policies as well as external and security policies. Therefore, only rather pragmatic suggestions are made envisaging more effective common actions[153]).

(b) A pragmatic and perhaps more realistic way of simplifying the Union's architecture is to adapt the second and third pillars to the most pressing de-mands, which concern the role of the Parliament and the Courts.

The *Commission* not only points at problems of interpretation and gives support to the EP's claims for formal consultation prior to any decision taken, but also makes a distinction between CFSP on the one hand and JHA on the other. With respect to the latter it asks for "a greater degree of parliamentary control especially where binding legal instruments are involved", since these questions are likely to have "a direct effect on individuals' basic rights and public freedoms"[154]). The *EP* asks for shared democratic accountability be-tween itself and national parliaments for matters which do not form part of the first pillar[155]). It also wants the roles of the ECJ, the Court of Auditors, and its own role strengthened "in those areas where there is currently inadequate scru-tiny at European level" (CFSP, EMU, JHA)[156]). The ECJ's competence should

---

[150]) CES 273/95 fin, pt. I.5.10.

[151]) Guéna Report (French Senate) 1995, 9.

[152]) Guéna Report (French Senate) 1995, 43 f.

[153]) Europäische Strukturkommission 1994, 44 ff.

[154]) Commission Report, SEC(95) 731, 14.

[155]) EP Resolution from 17. 5. 1995, PE 190.441, pt. 3.iii.

[156]) EP Resolution from 17. 5. 1995, PE 190.441, pt. 4 and 23.iv.

be extended to these areas[157]). The *ECJ* itself also requests an extension of its competencies to the areas covered by the second and third pillars[158]). The *FT Round Table* argues that the ECJ should have jurisdiction in the field of the second pillar "at least where the rights of individuals are affected, and perhaps as regards the fulfilment of Treaty procedures and obligations as well." Concerning JHA it simply sees "no valid justification for excluding the Court from these fields."[159])

- An Austrian Perspective

Along with most of the other European states, Austria is a polity with a written constitution. The 'Bundes-Verfassungsgesetz' (B-VG) sets out in a logically structured and comprehensive manner the foundation of a federal state. Although it is widely admitted that after some 75 years of experience and practice the Austrian basic law does not reflect political reality in all respects any more, it still gave a fairly accurate picture of at least the formal rules which constitute the point of reference for the political processes until very recently. One of the constitutional preconditions for Austrian EU membership was a positive referendum, as joining the Union meant a fundamental change of the Constitution ('Gesamtänderung'). Consequently, the Bundes-Verfassungsgesetz was amended in order to adapt it to the new political situation within an integrated Europe. There is now a new section on the European Union (Articles 23a to 23f B-VG) which contains provisions for the election or appointment of the Austrian members to the EC institutions; rules on the participation of the federate states ('Länder') and the local level in the decision-making process at the federal level concerning EU affairs; rules on Austria's participation in CFSP; and, very importantly, on the relationship between the Austrian representatives in the EU Council of Ministers and the Austrian Parliament ('Nationalrat')[160]). However, two important features cannot be deducted from the Austrian Constitution any more: first, how the majority of those decisions which are directly applicable or which have to be transposed into the Austrian legal order are actually taken; and second, what the remaining competencies of

---

[157]) EP Resolution from 17. 5. 1995, PE 190.441, pt. 25.i.

[158]) ECJ Report from May 1995, pt. 4.

[159]) Federal Trust Papers N° 3, 26.

[160]) Article 23e B-VG introduces a system of binding the Minister's behaviour to an opinion of the Nationalrat similar to the Danish system (see below III.B.2.f.1).

the Austrian legislator are. These rules are to be found in the Treaties, establishing the Union and its Communities, which were published in the Austrian Official Journal. They are linked only marginally to the Austrian Constitution because they partly have the status of constitutional laws and are therefore applicable in the same way as the 'old' Constitution. A second link is provided by a new constitutional law providing that the Adhesion Treaty is (formally) compatible with the Bundes-Verfassungsgesetz. Summing up, we may conclude that the Austrian Constitution — which until recently contained at least definite rules on the distribution of competencies between all relevant layers of government — was virtually replaced by a constitutional patchwork which makes it considerably more difficult than before to find out who can do what and how that affects the lives of the Austrians.

This situation could be improved by clearing the ground at the European level. As has been argued by many (see above), the 'constitutional' framework of the Union lacks coherence, logic, and accessibility since it has been amended several times over a period of some forty years. The widespread anti-European feelings which are reported by recent opinion polls are based not only on some of the policy outcomes of the Union but also on the remoteness of the 'Brussels system' hidden behind a 'forest' of unclear and intransparent rules. Considering this, an effort to improve the constitutional situation seems to be a highly rewarding task. All provisions which for various reasons are not applicable any more should be deleted; the structure of the treaty/constitution should be designed in a way to make it readable also an ordinary citizen; every Article should get an official title in order to make it more accessible.

We suggest not sticking too much to the labels of 'constitution' or 'treaty'. In fact, it cannot be denied that the legal framework of the Union and the Communities already fulfils some of the major tasks of a constitution: looking at the role of the ECJ, the issue of fundamental rights, the relationship between the national and the European law, the notion of 'new legal order' as used by the Court, etc., we have to conclude that the process of constitutionalising began a long time ago and is still under way incrementally. There is only a small dividing line between a treaty and a constitution, it is probably much more a matter of form and presentation than content. There is no list of items which have to be dealt with in a 'genuine' constitution[161]).

---

[161]) It could be argued that the fundamental difference between a 'constitution' on the one hand, and a 'treaty' on the other could be the way future amendments are being processed.

However, calling what will happen in 1996 'the drafting of a European Constitution' might well play an important role in getting the attention of the European citizens — something which, in turn, might positively influence the ratification process. The writing of a 'constitution' could be used to seek assent on some European fundamental principles which should, in turn, guide future development. The future fundamental text of the Union should set out for example the principle of democracy and the rule of law.

The same is true for the question of fundamental human and social rights, which can — despite all political and legal obstacles — not be left out in a text that aims at serving as a reference point for human identities.

Finally, considering the future of the three-pillar system, it seems strongly advisable to merge at least the first and third pillars. Furthermore, there is no convincing reason to exclude foreign and security policy from democratic and judicial control, as is still the case now. Obviously, the restriction of this area to governmental policy and therefore to intergovernmental bargaining corresponds to some historical traditions, but it is not compatible with a modern straightforward policy of democratisation of the Union and should therefore be abolished. However, different decision-making rules for highly sensible areas could still be applicable (e.g. unanimity or opt-outs if a Member state is outvoted within CFSP; see below).

There are two alternatives: either by 'internal' institutions and procedures, i.e. by the Council and/or the Parliament, or by 'external' negotiations involving only the institutions of the Member states, i.e. the sub-units of the European system. We suggest that the present system for constitutional amendments at the EU level is somewhere in between these two extremes and moving towards the first alternative. First, there is Article 235 ECT which allows for an incremental transfer of competencies from the Member states to the Community level, at least to a certain extent (argumentum "within the objective of the Community"). Second, the EU institutions are increasingly getting involved in the debates preceding amendments (see the reports to, and participation in, the Reflection Group as well as the mediating role of the Commission in the IGC). As soon as this de facto consultative function is changed into a right of assent for the European Parliament to all 'constitutional amendments' (as the EP proposes), it would be very difficult to say whether we are in the presence of a 'constitution', or still of a traditional 'treaty', despite all labelling. In our view, in this case the dividing line would be transgressed, even when the institutions of the Member states would continue to ratify the amendments also assented by the EP.

b) Flexibility Within Unity: Variations In European Integration?

The perspective of a possible doubling of Member states in the near future, bringing about increased structural diversity, has made the subject of differentiation within the project of European integration ever more topical. The number of different concepts which have to be mentioned here can be placed on a continuum extending between the poles of unity on the one hand, and flexibility on the other.

(1) The Models

The most 'unitarian' solution would clearly be one where all 'common' policies are conducted by all members of the Community jointly, such as within the old European Economic Community. Thus, no flexibility in terms of participation in principle, or even in time, is allowed for. Clearly, co-operation outside the European Communities has been going on between some of the Member states for a long time already (e.g. European Monetary System, Schengen Agreement). However, the concept of a rather unitarian Community has finally been given up even in terms of primary EC law at Maastricht, where opt-outs from goals and targets agreed on by the others were granted to the UK and Denmark.

Within a more flexible model of European integration, three criteria are useful for categorisation: *goals* (are they shared by all Member states or not?), *speed* of goal achievement (are some members given more time than others for reaching specific goals?), and *independence* for single members concerning opting-in or opting-out (only in groups, at any time?).

Within the extremely flexible option of a '*Europe à la carte*' or '*pick and choose Europe*', each Member state decides individually in which policy area given on the 'menu' it wants to participate, without in principle being concerned by any effects or costs of the others (no common goal, maximal flexibility for the single Member state). A first step towards this strategy is the opt-out of the UK from the social policy innovations of the Maastricht Treaty. In other words, Europe à la carte would be a generalised 'Social Protocol' model. In its most far-reaching variant, this model would allow for national choices to be reversed at any given point in time, subject only to prior notification to the European partners (and not only in IGCs).

In contrast, a '*Europe of several speeds*' or '*multiple tracks*' implies that all Member states jointly decide which policies to pursue (common goals), but then allow for temporary derogations for those members which cannot or do not want to proceed at the same speed as others. Economic and monetary union, as provided for in the respective chapter of the Maastricht Treaty, is an example of such a strategy[162]), and the same is true for the tradition of granting transitional periods to new Member states.

Between those two options of 'pick and choose' (maximum flexibility concerning goals and participants) and 'Europe of multiple speeds (or tracks)', several more concepts may be located. Thus, a *'hard core'* of EU Member states (or 'Kerneuropa') implies that an inner circle of countries would participate in all policy areas which are included in the Treaties, while the other members which cannot or do not want to do so would constitute less involved layers 'around' them. The notion of *'variable geometry'*, on the other hand, is slightly more cohesive as all Member states would have to participate in some European policies, but for further fields of European activity, diverse groups of members could participate (without, however, as much flexibility for individual members as in the model of 'pick and choose'). In a nutshell: 'hard core' means that some members participate in all policies, whereas 'variable geometry' implies that all members participate in some specific areas. Clearly, those concepts are not mutually exclusive but focus on different aspects of an outlined situation.

One model which does not smoothly fit into the concept outlined above is that of several *circles*. It was primarily promoted in the early 1990s by the former Commission President *Jacques Delors*, and concerns the dimension of external relations of the Union with other European states. Delors de facto tried to prevent a further widening of the EC before the Internal Market was completed, and wanted to at least postpone applications by the northern European states and Austria (who are meanwhile — except for Norway — EC members). Thus, he suggested that around the central circle of EC Member states, other layers would follow, such as the one of the European Economic Area (initially suggested to provide an alternative for membership to the EFTA states) and that of the 'Europe Agreements' with the former Soviet bloc members in central and eastern Europe. While no exceptions within one circle would be allowed, the states could move on from one circle to another when time was ripe.

---

162) However, the British and later the Danish managed to be granted the possibility to *opt-out* in Protocols to the Treaty.

If we look at the diverse proposals put forward within the ongoing reform debate, the last part of a quote[163]) by *John Major* might well stick in ones mind: "The fact is that there are not *two* approaches to Europe among Governments of the Union, but one and twelve. *One* because we are all firmly committed to a strong and effective European Union. But *twelve* because no two Governments have identical approaches."[164]) What makes the overview on the present state of the debate and the national positions even more difficult is the fact that the notions outlined above often appear in diluted forms, or are even applied unsystematically.

(2) Political Standpoints

The clearest choice of all might be attributed to the present *British government*: By arguing that greater flexibility was the only way in which it was possible to build a Union rising to 16 and ultimately to 20 or more Member states, the Prime Minister promoted the concept of pick-and-choose Europe, where each government could decide whether or not to participate in any given European policy, but everybody should be allowed to participate everywhere. For him, the "real danger" is "in talk of a 'hard core', inner and outer circles, a two-tier Europe, (...) a union in which some would be more equal than others. There is not, and should never be, an exclusive hard core either of countries or of policies."[165])

So far, those options have been rejected by most *other governments* who came forward with proposals concerning the management of increasing variety within the Union, for example the German (CDU/CSU paper, see immediately below), the French[166]), the Belgians[167]), and the Spanish[168]). They all pro-

---

[163]) As opposed to the second which is a more solemn than serious sentence.

[164]) *John Major*, Speech at the University of Leiden, 7 September 1994, p. 2 of manuscript.

[165]) *John Major*, Speech at the University of Leiden, 7 September 1994, p. 6 of manuscript.

[166]) According to the Minister for European affairs, during December 1994, France "rejects an à la carte Europe, which would be the opposite of European solidarity" (*Lamassour* cited by Agence Europe, 9 December 1994, 4).

[167]) Despite the fact that, considering the increased divergence in an ever larger Union, some kind of differentiation might be useful, a 'Europe à la carte# was nothing *Belgium* could favour (Belgian Prime Minister, *Jean-Luc Dehaene*, see Agence Europe, 20 January 1995, 3).

moted some variant of a hard core of members or a variable geometry including a "hard core"[169]) of policies where everybody should participate. In many cases, the upholding of a single institutional framework was advocated.

Even if the *CDU/CSU paper* is not explicitly decided on the choice of a variable geometry or a multi-speed model, it is strongly opposed to 'Europe à la carte'. In order to avoid any drifting apart of the different regions of an ever bigger Union, the *CDU/CSU* proposes the strengthening of a 'hard core' of Member states, i.e. France and Germany as an 'inner core' and the Benelux countries. These countries should not only participate in all Union policies but also act more closely and more Union-oriented than others, and should be the motor of initiatives, especially in the field of the new Maastricht policies such as monetary, fiscal, economic, and social policies[170]). However, the paper is not very precise in terms of how to put this into practice and how to organise the relationship with the other Member states which are not part of the hard core.

In a much debated interview with Les Echos[171]), the former Commission President *Jacques Delors* outlined his conception of a "federation of states" between a core of European countries. Adopting a German rather than a traditional French interpretation of federalism, he stated that for him the "federal approach is the one which guarantees the least centralisation of powers and the greatest democratic control"[172]). The 'Federation of European states' should be built among those who "think that without a single currency and without a common defence we will not succeed in guaranteeing our independence, preserving our standard of living and restoring our influence in the world" (ibid.). He locates this 'Federation' as the inner circle of a 'Europe of thirty' with a more limited scope of competencies than the existing EU and with an adapted institutional system. The 'Federation' should be built upon a treaty with clear

---

[168]) See reports on government statements, e.g. in Agence Europe, 11 February 1995, 3; 11 March 1995, 4 f.

[169]) Attention: This 'hard core' (of policies) has clearly nothing to do with the 'hard core' (of Member states) of the CDU/CSU paper!

[170]) CDU/CSU September 1994, 7 f.

[171]) 6 December 1994; see also Agence Europe 9 December 1994, 1.

[172]) Les Echos, 6 December 1994; English quotation from Agence Europe 9 December 1994, 1.

definition of the sharing of sovereignty and the protection of nations, and be open to all those who agree to comply with the duties and obligations of this treaty.

Without explicitly talking about a federation of core states, other French politicians such as *Jacques Chirac*[173]) and *Edouard Balladur*[174]), have also promoted a Europe of several circles, partly while underlining that institutional unity has to be protected[175]). In autumn 1994, *Balladur* suggested a Europe of three circles, one of them being CSCE, including countries which would not be members, at least for a long time. The middle circle would accordingly be the current Union based on the Maastricht Treaty, and the inner one a more structured organisation "sur le plan monetaire comme sur le plan militaire"[176]). Some months later, however, his outline allowed for even more flexibility: "We should move forward with those who can and want to do so in each area where progress is necessary — currency, defence, internal security amongst others. We shall thus build circles of stronger co-operation which will not necessarily group together the same member States on each subject."[177]) For France, there is thus a development towards more flexibility to be observed: In April 1994, the French Minister for European Affairs, *Lamassoure*, had still elaborated measures in order to create a contagious effect on the other Member states, i.e. giving them an incentive to participate in all the Union's policies. Thus, he suggested attributing the status of "new founder members" to all who entered into the third phase of EMU and participated in all other policy areas[178]).

The *Spanish* government has on several occasions stated that some flexibility in the sense of 'variable geometry' was inevitable[179]), but that there should not be any irreversible exclusion, on the one hand, or a 'pick-and-choose Europe' on the other. This government therefore opts for a solution of variable geometry (which is also called scenario of "reinforced solidarity") which nonetheless should be a last resort only; maintain all acquis communautaire; have

---

173) See Agence Europe, 23 March 1995, 2.

174) See Agence Europe, 30 December 1995, 1 f.

175) So Minister for European Affairs, *Lamassoure*, Agence Europe, 1 February 1995, 3.

176) Le Figaro, 30 August 1994.

177) Cited from Agence Europe, 30 December 1994, 1.

178) See Agence Europe, 18 April 1994, 7.

179) See Agence Europe, 11 February 1995, 3; 11 March 1995, 4 f.

the core in principle open to all Member states; be compatible with the idea of a community of law founded on a single institutional framework; and provide for flanking policies for strengthening the overall coherence of the Union, and allow real convergence of those lagging behind[180]). However, nothing should prevent any country from leaving the hard core.

The *Commission* took the stance that the concept of different speeds of integration was nothing "unusual" in the past, somewhat tactically referring also to the Schengen Agreement, which, in fact, is rather part of a 'variable geometry' set-up (it is a co-operation outside the Treaties among some Member states only). Thus, this concept could also be used in the future provided that it happens in a single institutional framework and be centred on a common objective[181]). As the Commissioner for Constitutional Questions recently put it:

> "Even when a policy only concerns a minority of Member states, institutional unity should not be affected, notably regarding the Parliament's role of political control which should extend to all areas of co-operation."[182])

Concerning an à la carte Europe (defined as permanent exemptions), the Commission obviously regrets that this exists at the moment at least in the case of the social policy[183]), and strongly opposes any such concepts for the future.

The *EP* also rejects the option of a 'pick-and-choose Europe'. In fact, one of several conditions set out by Parliament is that any flexible arrangements due to increasing diversity of the EU should not lead to the possibility of individual pick-and-choose. Furthermore, such arrangements must, according to the EP, not undermine the single institutional framework; the acquis communautaire; the principles of solidarity and economic and social cohesion throughout the European Union; as well as "the principle of equality of all States and citizens of the Union before the Treaty"[184]). The control "over those Union policies which are pursued by a limited number of Member states on a temporary basis" (a formulation which indicates that the EP in fact prefers a more

---

[180]) Paper of the Spanish Government called "The 1996 Conference — bases for discussion", cited from Agence Europe, 11 March 1995, 4 f.

[181]) Commission Report, SEC(95) 731, 6.

[182]) *Marcelino Oreja Aguirre*, AE 26. 4. 1995, 4.

[183]) Commission Report, SEC(95) 731, 6.

[184]) EP Resolution from 17. 5. 1995, PE 190.441, pt. 15.

cohesive multiple speed solution only) should be exercised by the European Parliament as a whole[185]).

The *ESC* does not address the problem as a whole but calls strongly for the abolition of opt-outs in social matters[186]).

(3) Expert and Scholarly Viewpoints

If we turn to the expert contributions to the reform debate, a "Europe à la carte" is again rejected by the majority. Even the *European Constitutional Group* provides for a core area of policies without opt-outs:

> "The rules and procedures for acting together in each area of the constitution shall allow for individual members to dissent with the exception of those obligations accepted by qualified majorities as necessary to maintain free and open markets. In cases where members 'opt out' of a policy area, they shall have no votes in that area"[187]).

With the provision that any new Member state may avail itself of such arrangements as are available to any existing Member state outside the fields of free movement of goods, services, and capital in the internal market[188]), the present British opt-out from social policy measures by the other Member states, which is heavily criticised for example by the Commission, would probably even be extended in scope with an Eastern enlargement to come.

In contrast, *Ludlow/Ersbøll* reject any 'Europe à la carte' model, even if moderated, because it

> "reduces the essential obligations of EU membership to a bare minimum, thereby destroying many of the essential linkages that underpin the present package and reducing the single institutional framework to a marginal role."[189])

They also dismiss the 'hard core' model because it might have a similar effect as the former "since the single institutional framework would in practice

---

[185]) EP Resolution from 17. 5. 1995, PE 190.441, pt. 16.

[186]) CES 273/95 fin, pt. I.5.7.

[187]) European Constitutional Group 1993, 2a, p. 5.

[188]) European Constitutional Group 1993, 2a, p. 5.

[189]) *Ludlow/Ersbøll* (CEPS) 1995, 56.

be reserved for 'lesser' business and the obligations, let alone the rights of weaker states, would be bound to be reduced if not to totally disappear"[190]). *Ludlow/ Ersbøll* develop five guiding principles for any recommendable path towards more diversity: (1) opting in should be the norm, opting out the exception; (2) all Member states should participate in the single institutional framework; (3) those who opt out should have less than full rights in the institutions in relation to the business in which they do not intend to participate; (4) they should be obliged to accept the majority's 'droit de regard', including the right of their partners to define their own non-conformity as destabilising or unacceptable; (5) the Treaty should incorporate detailed provisions to deal with unacceptable or destabilising behaviour in articles that apply across the board[191]). They suggest making opting-out a 'normal business', and not placing the onus on those who opt out will inevitably tend to dilute the notion of the Union and reduce it in due course to no more than an association of states[192]).

'Charlemagne' specifically elaborate on a 'pick-and choose model' (although they call it a model of variable geometry)[193]). The paper argues that all Member states should have to participate at a "socle commun minimum", a minimum core of common policies. While the inner core of these policies (namely the internal market, the four freedoms, the competition and common commercial policies, and CAP in as much as it is necessary for the free movement of goods) seems to be rather undisputed, other areas are considered to have important effects on competition, namely transport, fiscal, environmental, social, and industrial policies. They should consequently be part of the minimum core[194]). Shortcomings of flexible models would be the primacy of those policies carried out by all Member states over those of only a group of states. Further problems concern the external competencies *vis-à-vis* third countries and the functioning of the institutions in those fields without overall Union competence. *'Charlemagne'* differentiate between those institutions which carry out their tasks in whole independence and in the general interest of the Union, such as the Commission and the Courts (and possibly the EP), on the one hand, and the Council, on the other. For the first group the paper advocates contin-

---

[190]) *Ludlow/Ersbøll* (CEPS) 1995, 56.

[191]) *Ludlow/Ersbøll* (CEPS) 1995, 56 f.

[192]) *Ludlow/Ersbøll* (CEPS) 1995, 57.

[193]) *'Charlemagne'*, October 1994, p. 71 ff.

[194]) *'Charlemagne'*, October 1994, p. 72.

ued participation of those nationals whose Member states opted out for a specific policy[195]) — which corresponds to the current practice in social policy. Finally, any variable geometry must, in the eyes of '*Charlemagne*', respect the acquis communautaire without stepping back[196]).

'*Justus Lipsius*', too, considers that only a variable geometry allows to meet the challenge to "impose a reform of the EU structures and procedures, the aim of which will be not to jeopardise the efficiency of the EU decision-making process, while allowing some of its Member states to go ahead towards more integration without being prevented from doing so by the other Member states which do not want or which cannot follow them"[197]). In contrast, he judges the concept of multi-track Europe to be insufficient to solve the problems which will arise — implying that among a group of almost thirty members, it might well not be possible to find agreement on common goals in all important areas, even if temporary derogations be permitted. A Europe à la carte is simply not "conceivable" to him "because it would be unable to provide for the necessary balance between rights and obligations among all Member states because it would entail distortions of competition, negate the concept of a single market, prevent the EU from acting as a single entity in the outside world, etc."[198]). However, the possibility of a variable geometry, '*Lipsius*' judges to be interesting and, despite the limits and difficulties it could raise, necessary. He recommends a number of principles be respected (which correspond with those suggested by aforementioned authors): A single institutional framework should exist, even if its functioning would have to be adapted in some policy fields where not all members participate. "A large, thick, strong, common base"[199]) should incorporate all policies in which divergences between Member states could give rise to significant distortions of competition, and even for the optional policies outside of these common core policies, a minimum of rules should be mandatory, so that derogations never be full and/or absolute. Moreover, '*Lipsius*' suggests that the Treaty provide for the possibility of adopting compensatory measures in cases of distortion of competition because of non-

---

[195]) '*Charlemagne*', October 1994, p. 74 ff.

[196]) '*Charlemagne*', October 1994, p. 77 f.

[197]) '*Justus Lipsius*' 1995, 14.

[198]) '*Justus Lipsius*' 1995, 15.

[199]) '*Justus Lipsius*' 1995, 16.

participation. A rule of non-interference should guarantee that particular co-operations may not affect common policies.

To sum up, there seems a certain opinion leadership for models of 'variable geometry' and possibly a 'hard core' which nonetheless respect both the acquis communautaire and the integrity of European integration in terms of external representation and internal cohesion.

(4) Let-Out-Clause

One way of solving at least some of the problems of different aspirations and perceptions concerning the further development of the Union could be the introduction of a so-called let-out-clause. There are two aspects to this.

First, the predicted complications with the United Kingdom during the IGC, because this country seems the most reluctant at the moment to take considerable steps forward with the other states on the path of further integration. *Parliament* suggests that consideration be given to proceeding without the minority if at the IGC '96, "despite broad agreement among a majority of Member states and peoples of the European Union" no unanimous decision can be reached. This could be made effective by "instruments to enable a Member state to leave the EU, subject to meeting certain criteria"[200]).

The other aspect concerns mainly the perspective of further enlargement, as among the next candidates are some with a very weak and short democratic tradition. Since the attachment to the 'principles of democracy' is a criterion of membership (Article F TEU), *Ludlow/Ersbøll* address the question of what happens if, as a result of regime change, a Member state starts to breach these principles[201]). One solution would obviously be to cease its membership. More generally even, under the proposed EU charter of the *European Constitutional Group*, "any Member state may decide to leave the Union under procedures that meet its own constitutional requirements"[202]). On the other hand, if a state ceases its membership in the Council of Europe on the grounds of violation of its Convention on Human Rights it shall also cease to be a member of the Union[203]).

---

[200]) EP Resolution from 17. 5. 1995, PE 190.441, pt. 17.

[201]) *Ludlow/Ersbøll* (CEPS) 1995, 35.

[202]) European Constitutional Group 1993, 2c, p. 5.

[203]) European Constitutional Group 1993, 2c, p. 5.

- An Austrian Perspective

When Austria joined the Union, the latter was still a quite unitarian entity except for the limited opt-outs concerning social policy and future defence options. Since Austria is an advanced social market economy with relatively high social, environmental, and consumer standards, we think that there exists a strong interest in preventing any 'pick and choose' model which would necessarily imply distortion of competition while completely open markets have to be maintained. As far as policies in fields which do not affect conditions of competition — such as monetary unity or defence — are concerned, however, things indeed do look different. In the longer run, a certain degree of flexibility might in such areas even bear uniting impact, allowing for innovations first to be tested among a few only. Therefore, comparatively more flexibility seems to be acceptable in this respect from an Austrian point of view.

Whatever the specific model of increased flexibility then adopted, from an Austrian perspective the main condition should be that there is a certain core of activities which all Member states share, clearly centred around the internal market and its flanking policies. Thus, the so-called 'horizontal' policies such as social, environmental, and consumer policies have to be part of the inner core of common Union activities. In this view the British opt-out in the field of social policy as well as any model granting similar opportunities to other (also future) Member states is unacceptable. Only around the present acquis communautaire in the wider sense, might a 'variable geometry' allow those countries which want to do so, proceed further with additional policy areas. Clearly, a model involving a 'hard core' of countries within that might provide a comparatively higher degree of coherence and seems therefore more appropriate to possibly attract all members at a later point in time, so that full coherence within the Union could be re-established. Until then, the single institutional framework should be maintained and no stepping back behind the present acquis communautaire should be allowed.

c) Division of Competencies Between EU and Member States

So far, the delimitation of the respective spheres of activity between the Union legislator and the Member states, as laid down in the Treaties, is rather an allocation of functions than a concrete and unambiguous division of competencies. Although European lawyers used to call it a system of 'single authorisations' ('*Einzelermächtigungen*'), meaning that the supranational level can only act if there is a specific authorisation to be found in the Treaties, some of these authorisations are quite comprehensive and allow for a very broad range of activities (Articles 100a and 235 ECT). In the past, the Union legislator tended to make extensive use of these wide competencies. The principle of subsidiarity in Articles A EUT and 3b ECT was introduced at the last IGC in order to counter-balance this tendency towards centralisation. Article A affirms that "decisions are taken as closely as possible to the people"; Article 3b makes the principle more operational by requiring the Community to act only where the objectives

> "cannot be sufficiently achieved by the Member states and can therefore, by reason of the scale or effects of the proposed action, be better achieved by the Community."

However, the political as well as academic discourse since the entry into force of the EUT, made it clear that this compromise formula fell short of solving the problem of division of competencies in a quasi-federal setting such as the EU. Therefore the issue is very likely to be on the agenda of the IGC '96.

The *Europäische Strukturkommission* for instance argues that the subsidiarity principle as formulated in Article 3b ECT cannot suffice the demands because it does not provide clear enough criteria for the division of competencies, but leaves the decision to actors (Commission, governments) which cannot be expected to always apply it systematically and in a restrictive manner[204]. In contrast, a detailed catalogue of competencies ("*Kompetenzkatalog*") should, according to the Europäische Strukturkommission, describe the existing division of competencies as transparently as possible, and provide principles for further transfers as well as for the exercise of competencies. Clearly, the aim of the Europäische Strukturkommission is a stable distribution of competencies contrasting what they see as the traditional trend towards ever more supranational policies. Therefore, its detailed catalogue of competencies[205] attributes in the case of all major policy areas *primary* and *partial competencies* to either the Union or the Member states. For example, foreign policy, security and military are suggested as primary competencies of the Member states, with partial competencies of the Union (called CFSP) including co-ordination, mu-

---

[204]) Europäische Strukturkommission 1994, 17.

[205]) Europäische Strukturkommission 1994, 20 ff.

tual information, common actions and implementation decisions[206]). On the other hand, for example fisheries and agricultural policies are suggested as primary competencies of the Union, while national structural policies in the agricultural area are mentioned as partial competency for the Member states. In general, primary competencies of one level should allow only for interventions by the other level if an explicit enumerative partial competency has been provided. In the absence of subsidiary competence provisions like Article 235 ECT, any further transfer of additional competencies would only work with ratification by the Member states. An interesting detail about this proposal is the inherent criticism that the EC interfere with competencies of the Member states via financial incentives, for example in the fields of education, health, or culture[207]). Therefore, restrictive enumeration of eligible financial transfers is suggested: The desire for European financial resources should not be a determining criteria for the transfer of competencies in the long term. Furthermore, the Europäische Strukturkommission wants to submit the Union to a generalised principle of loyalty, including the respect of internal national structures within the exercise of Union policies[208]).

Although the *FT Round Table* argues that such a catalogue of competencies would "require very thorough preparation, by what would amount to a constitutional conference" and therefore concludes that "it is not a matter for the forthcoming IGC"[209]), the proposal of the Europäische Strukturkommission has been welcomed by some commentators: The *CDU/CSU paper* endorses the idea of a strict list of competencies[210]) and also the *German Bundesrat* requests a list of the Union's competencies[211]). While agreeing with the idea of a 'Kompetenzkatalog' as proposed by the Europäische Strukturkommission in principle, *Ludlow/Ersbøll* argue that it should not be accompanied by a total elimination of Article 235 ECT:

> "[I]n any healthy polity there must be room for the interplay of political forces to redefine the frontiers between the different levels of government as an[d] when circumstances change. Something like

---

[206]) Europäische Strukturkommission 1994, 20.

[207]) Europäische Strukturkommission 1994, 27.

[208]) Europäische Strukturkommission 1994, 29.

[209]) FT Trust Paper N° 6, 28.

[210]) CDU/CSU September 1994, 5.

[211]) Agence Europe, 1 April 1995, 3.

Article 235, remodelled perhaps to allow a stronger role for the European Parliament through the introduction of co-decision procedures, would therefore seem to be indispensable."[212])

Also the *EP* wants to retain Article 235 ECT, but use it only as a last resort and after assent of the EP[213]). In contrast, the *ESC* proposes that the co-operation procedure should be used, and that consultation of the ESC should also be mandatory[214]). The *EP* suggests that the IGC should primarily concentrate not on transferring new powers to the EU institutions, but on clarifying their respective roles[215]). Also *'Justus Lipsius'* wants to keep Article 235 because it is still necessary for example to set up new organs; but he proposes the co-decision procedure and even wants to delete the reference to the Common Market in that provision. He seems to be rather conservative in the area of competencies and thinks that a catalogue of competencies would be too difficult to establish[216]).

Another route would be the further elaboration of the principle of subsidiarity, either in combination with the drafting of the 'Kompetenzkatalog', such as the *German Bundesrat* requests[217]), or without this. For example *John Major* announced his intention to "block any attempt to extend Community competence to inter-governmental areas such as foreign affairs, defence and home affairs", and his determination to "aim to strengthen subsidiarity which has already led to a reduction in Commission activity"[218]). In contrast, the *Spanish* government has stressed that a more explicit definition of the subsidiarity principle might even be a negative thing[219]). Spain recalls that during the Maastricht IGC, it had presented a memorandum on an alternative principle, that of "sufficient means". Clearly, Spain will be a defender of the acquis communautaire and the competencies of the supranational institutions.

---

[212]) *Ludlow/Ersbøll* (CEPS) 1995, 16.

[213]) EP Resolution from 17. 5. 1995, PE 190.441, pt. 12.ii.

[214]) CES 273/95 fin, pt. I.9.

[215]) EP Resolution from 17. 5. 1995, PE 190.441, pt. 18.

[216]) *'Justus Lipsius'* 1995, 41.

[217]) Agence Europe, 1 April 1995, 3.

[218]) *Major* cited from Agence Europe, 25 May 1995, 2.

[219]) Paper of the Spanish Government called "The 1996 Conference — bases for discussion", cited from Agence Europe, 11 March 1995, 4 f.

The *European Constitutional Group's* visions, on the other hand, do clearly favour the national vis-à-vis the supranational level. Thus, they want to see a restrictive catalogue of Community competencies, the abolishment of Article 235, and a strengthened subsidiarity principle:

> "Before voting on any bill or amended bill (...), the Chamber of Parliamentarians shall consider whether the end which the bill is calculated to secure can in principle instead be secured by the Member states, or by one or more of the Member states, or by one or more of the public authorities of the Member states, without recourse to the powers and institutions of the Union. If that end can be so secured, the Chamber shall not assent to the bill."[220]

The *European Constitutional Group* sets comparatively narrow limits upon the powers of the Union: without specific conditions for Union action being fulfilled, its bodies do not have any explicit powers[221]. Among the existing competencies of the Union, a number would have to be cancelled, for example in the fields of environmental protection and social policy. In cases where amendments to Union measures would, in the view of a qualified minority of the Chamber of Parliamentarians, pertain to the distribution of powers between the Member states and the Union, the final decision would lay with this Chamber consisting of national parliamentarians which are expected to protect national autonomy[222].

The *Spanish* government thinks in a partially similar direction: national parliaments should have the right to address complaints to the ECJ on the grounds of subsidiarity. K. Hänsch, the former EP President, obviously referring to the proposal of a Chamber of Parliamentarians, commented that: "This could be, under certain conditions, at least an improvement on the suggestion (...) [of a] Chamber of Subsidiarity"[223]. The *European Constitutional Group* elaborated on this proposal even more: if any of the judgements by the ECJ pertained to the distribution of powers, a Member state or a qualified majority of the Chamber of Parliamentarians might call for review of the adjudication by the

---

[220] European Constitutional Group 1993, Sec. 7. of the proposed constitution; as to the proposed 'Chamber of (national!) Parliamentarians' see chapter III.B.2.f.2.

[221] European Constitutional Group 1993, 3a, p. 71.

[222] European Constitutional Group 1993, 2c, p. 8.

[223] *Hänsch* 1995, 6.

Union Court of Review, consisting of representatives of national judiciaries[224]). Members of national judiciaries making up this additional Court shall therefore see that Union competencies are not exceeded, and that directly applicable Union law and the jurisdiction of the ECJ be very limited. They argue that a

> "system of diversified law is much more likely to offer protection to individuals and to a decentralised system of Union government than according a dominant role to a single Court such as the Court of Justice that has a vested interest in the extension of a single superior law."[225])

Concerning the role of the European Court of Justice and the principle of primacy of EC law, the proposal of the *European Constitutional Group* suggests that "the next Intergovernmental Conference must specifically reject the concept that there is a general hierarchy of authority to be developed in the Union"[226]). The Group does not mind that their "proposals in this area will be seen by some observers as challenging a significant part of the legal 'acquis'"[227]).

• An Austrian Perspective

Austria is a federal state where the competencies of the federal level (*'Bund'*) are listed in the Constitution and there is a general clause declaring that everything else falls within the competence of the federated states (*'Länder'*). The Austrian Constitutional Court watches over the legislative activity of the two levels and secures proper application. A similar system seems to be desirable for the relationship between the EU and the Member state levels because it could be much clearer and more transparent than the present system. Therefore, a 'Kompetenzkatalog' as proposed by the Europäische Strukturkommission, combined with the jurisdiction of the ECJ, is a highly convincing idea.

However, the principle of subsidiarity has worked quite well in political terms even though it has been criticised because it cannot be operationalised in legal terms (which is hardly surprising since it is a genuine political principle,

---

[224]) European Constitutional Group 1993, 2c, p. 9.

[225]) European Constitutional Group 1993, II, p. 3.

[226]) European Constitutional Group 1993, 2a, p. 3.

[227]) European Constitutional Group 1993, 2b, p. 13.

see below). Since Maastricht the Commission justifies its proposals and gives the reasons why it thinks the legislative act in question is adequate for regulation at the European level. Both Parliament and Council discuss the need of the act in terms of subsidiarity. Even though one might eventually argue that the EP, being a supranational institution, has no incentive to avoid legislation at the European level, the same can hardly be said of the Council of Ministers. The members of the latter represent not the Union's interests, but the Member states'. Furthermore, the ministers are politically dependent of their national parliaments which are the main losers in terms of competencies because of the activities at the supranational level. Therefore, there is no institution which is better equipped and in a more adequate political situation to watch that the principle of subsidiarity be applied with care. If we compare this situation with the Austrian second chamber at the federal level, which represents the Länder and has to approve any transfer of competencies to the federal level, we have to conclude that the latter is considerably weaker than the states' chamber at the EU level. Given these structural conditions and the experience of restrictive use of EC competencies during the past two years, one could argue that the project of a genuine 'Kompetenzkatalog' is not one of high priority. Nevertheless, the IGC should at least try to simplify the division of competencies in order to make it more transparent for the uninitiated citizen who wants to read and understand what the European polity is all about.

With respect to Article 235 ECT and its possible abolishment, we have to distinguish between two scenarios: the case of a catalogue of competencies to be drafted at the IGC, and the case of maintaining the present system with an eventually improved, i.e. clearer, principle of subsidiarity. Attribution of competencies is a political decision by its very nature. If the Member states could agree on a 'Kompetenzkatalog' now, the political decision would have been made and the issue turns into a matter of application, which can be supervised by the Court. In this case, Article 235 is not necessary any more. In the second scenario, the political decision is not taken at the IGC but postponed to the time of application of EU primary law. The specific translation of the subsidiarity principle takes place at the very moment of deciding on a legislative proposal, and it is necessarily a political decision (where is something achieved better?). Therefore Article 235 remains necessary since this provision contains the complimentary principle to the subsidiarity principle, i.e. the empowerment to act at the supranational level if this is judged desirable without there being a specific competency in the Treaties.

In terms of democratic principles and transparency, it seems therefore definitely better to sort things out at the IGC and to have a clear-cut catalogue of competencies[228]).

d) European Citizens and the Union

While the old European Economic Community treated the people as subjects to the Common Market and holders of some economic rights (such as the right to move freely within the Community), the TEU introduced European citizenship which acknowledged the special role of the citizens in the European polity, at least in principle. The European citizens have been granted some specific political rights, such as the right to vote and stand for local elections (see above II.B.3). However, the discussions following the adoption of the Maastricht Treaty at national level and the difficulties in the ratification processes made it clear that the demands of the citizens are much higher than anticipated by the European political elite. As the Commission recently put it:

> "[I]t is not certain that the Treaty has actually brought the Union closer to the general public (...)."[229])

The *European Parliament* calls for "greater substance" of the concept of EU citizenship through development of the special rights linked to it[230]). Obviously, there are many ways of achieving this. Some of them are being mentioned in other chapters, see for example the question of a fundamental rights catalogue (above III.B.1.a.1), the question of redrafting the Treaty framework in order to make it more accessible and readable for the uninitiated (above III.B.1.a), the uniform electoral procedure (below III.B.2.a), and the issue of secrecy in the Council and the wider issue of transparency (below III.B.3.e).

Only a few commentators actually discuss increased involvement of European citizens in the policy-making process itself. *Parliament* wants to develop "'political citizenship', inter alia through measures that facilitate participation

---

[228]) This could be accompanied by a specific procedure allowing for transfers of competencies without further IGCs, subject for example to assent of the EP. It should be mentioned, however, that this issues may be seen as crucial within the debate of whether the Union is a 'state' or an international ('sui generis') community (see also footnote 161 concerning the distinction between 'treaty' and 'constitution').

[229]) Commission Report, SEC(95) 731, 74; the Commission was, in particular, referring to "a shortage of openness in the field of justice and home affairs".

[230]) EP Resolution from 17. 5. 1995, PE 190.441, pt. 7.

in political life in a Member state of Union citizens residing in that State"[231]). Furthermore, it proposes a Union-wide referendum in order to ratify the outcome of the next IGC[232]) and calls for application and development of Article 138a ECT on European political parties "in order to develop the means of expression for citizens at European level"[233]). Although the *ESC* calls in its report for "grass-roots involvement in the integration process", for "opportunities and machinery for involvement in and supervision of the application of decisions" by the citizens, and for "a developing democratic and participatory society"[234]), it nevertheless sticks to mediated involvement when requesting mainly improvements for the ESC's participation in the decision-making. In contrast, the *European Constitutional Group* provides for the possibility of direct involvement of the citizens: "the group considered the need to have a means within the constitution for changing the fiscal limits. Here, an element of direct democracy for the tax payers is introduced in the constitution as additional tax payer protection"[235]).

- An Austrian Perspective

Far from being a 'semi-direct democracy', such as Switzerland or California, Austria's Constitution nevertheless provides, in places, for direct involvement of the citizens. There is an initiative process and a referendum device at the federal level, and public opinion polls both here and at the *Länder* level. In contrast, the European citizens do not have any opportunities for direct involvement and participation in the Union level decision-making. Any devices of direct democracy at the national level are practically neutralised at the European level since the decision-making rules do not take the outcome of such national popular decisions into account. Bearing in mind that, meanwhile, a substantive proportion of major decisions are being taken at that level, direct democracy has witnessed considerable decline by the very fact of EU membership.

---

[231]) EP Resolution from 17. 5. 1995, PE 190.441, pt. 7.

[232]) EP Resolution from 17. 5. 1995, PE 190.441, pt. 41 ff.

[233]) EP Resolution from 17. 5. 1995, PE 190.441, pt. 8.

[234]) CES 273/95 fin, pt. I.2, I.3.1 and I.3.2.

[235]) European Constitutional Group 1993, 2b, p. 17.

So far, the discussion of how to bring the citizens closer to the Union stayed very much on the surface of the problem. But enhancing legitimacy is part of a two-way process, it is not only about better informing the citizens of decisions which have already been taken (transparency), but — and perhaps even more important still — about actively involving the citizens in the decision-making. However important it is to consider how to 'sell' the products of European integration to the public, even more attention and closer reflection should be given to the content of the product, i.e. the design of the institutional and decision-making structure of the Union. Modern representative democracy has its roots in the principle of governance by the people through the people. Not least for the sake of social legitimacy, the authors of a new democratic European order are advised not to depart too far from the substance of democracy — notwithstanding any perfectly permissible and necessary considerations about efficiency of the decision-making structures.

A first step to consider would be a European-wide referendum on the outcome of the forthcoming IGC, because, without doubt, we are witnessing some process of 'state-building' in Europe. Keeping the addressees of the whole enterprise out of the process does not seem to be compatible with the very principles of democracy itself. In our opinion, further steps would have to follow. As we argue below, the right of initiative should be granted to other institutions (the Council, the PE, the national parliaments). Thinking about the possibility of a European-wide popular initiative could amend this system, creating the opportunity for the citizens to make Europe their cause.

2. Institutional Matters

In the following section we shall address to those questions which lie at the very heart of the debate on the democratic-deficit. We shall distinguish between institutional matters in the narrow sense, i.e. concerning the composition and structure of the institutions, and procedural questions, i.e. those more related to the legislative decision-making processes at Union level (see next section). Clearly, there are some topics which fall within both categories, especially the issue of institutional balance which is obviously determined by both organisational and procedural factors.

In general, 'institutional balance' is not explicitly mentioned in the various proposals[236]), but they add up clearly to affecting the balance. Thus, lets look first at the detailed discussions. We shall address here the following topics: the composition of the major institutions; the appointment procedures for Commissioner and other Union representatives; the future of the Presidency of the Council and the Union; the relationship between the EU system and national parliaments; and finally some proposals concerning the judicial system of the Union.

a) Composition of the European Parliament

Under this heading several aspects are being discussed: first, the number of MEPs, second the geographical distribution of seats, and third, the "old" subject of a uniform electoral procedure.

(i.) The size of the Parliament has increased considerably in recent years: in the first place because of German unity, and second because of the 1995 enlargement. It is widely considered that it has almost reached its maximal size, some even argue that the EP is too big already.

Therefore, fixing a maximum number of MEPs is under discussion. *'Justus Lipsius'* considers that, were the current method of attributing MEPs to Member states continued to a Union of 28, there would be almost 900 parliamentarians at the European level. In contrast, *'Lipsius'* suggests limiting the number "to 500 or a maximum of 600"[237]). The *EP* itself proposes a maximum number of 700 MEPs[238]), the *Guéna Report* the present number, i.e. 624[239]), *Europäische Strukturkommission* "significantly less than 700 members"[240]).

---

[236]) There are, however, some remarks on the position of the Commission to be found in this context: From the Belgian viewpoint, "the institutional equilibrium between the Council, the Commission, Parliament and the Court of Justice" is very much appreciated (Prime Minister *Dehaene*, cited from Agence Europe, 20 January 1995, 3). However, *Dehaene* pleaded in favour of further strengthening both the Commission and the EP. According to the Belgian Foreign Minister, *Frank Vandenbroucke*, the Commission should be considerably enhanced in order to "act like a true government" (Agence Europe, 16 January 1995, 4). In contrast, the President of the National Assembly in France, *Seguin*, asked in a much debated article in Le Figaro that the Commission be "re-centred, other than its role as guardian of the Treaties, on its role as administrative secretariat, proposal-making body and as executor of Council decisions" (Agence Europe, 8 December 1994, 5).

[237]) *'Justus Lipsius'* 1995, 25 f.

[238]) EP Resolution from 17. 5. 1995, PE 190.441, pt. 22.i.

(ii.) Fixing a maximum number can not only be seen in terms of guaranteeing sensible and efficient working conditions for the Parliament. *Ludlow/Ersbøll* address the other aspect inherent to the composition of the EP which is the relationship between representation and population numbers: "The present over-representation of Luxembourg voters and under-representation of German voters is clearly unsustainable in a longer term perspective, in which Luxembourg itself will cease to be the smallest state (...)"[241]. The *Guéna Report* proposes to use future enlargements to progressively review the numbers of MEPs of every Member state in order to come closer to demographic realities[242]. *'Justus Lipsius'* also wants to examine the guarantee of better representation of the people "while maintaining an overall better representation for the populations of the less populated smaller Member states and ensuring an equal representation between countries classified in the same 'category' in terms of population (for instance, countries with less than 1 or 2 million inhabitants, countries with more than 50 million ...)"[243]. Finally, *'Justus Lipsius'* wants to see a better proportionality between populations and numbers of MEPs of a country, "while maintaining an overall better representation for people in the less populated Member states and ensuring an equal representation between countries classified in the same 'category'" (in the sense of small, medium, large)[244].

(iii.) Talking about Parliament's composition, the issue of eventually deciding on the uniform electoral procedure has been mentioned in various contributions. Actually, this is nothing to be decided at an IGC: Article 138 ECT as amended by the TEU provides for a unanimous decision in the Council and the assent of the Parliament itself. The unanimity rule has prevented, so far, any consensus. Interestingly, the EP's resolution does not call for changing the rules for adoption of the electoral procedure[245]. Despite the existing decision

---

[239]) Guéna Report (French Senate) 1995, 23.

[240]) Europäische Strukturkommission 1994, 38.

[241]) *Ludlow/Ersbøll* (CEPS) 1995, 49.

[242]) Guéna Report (French Senate) 1995, 23.

[243]) *'Justus Lipsius'* 1995, 25 f.

[244]) *'Justus Lipsius'* 1995, 36.

[245]) EP Resolution from 17. 5. 1995, PE 190.441, pt. 22.iii.

rules, the issue could be tabled at the IGC alongside the overall assessment and reform of the composition of the EP, as outlined above.

'Justus Lipsius' reminds that agreeing on a uniform procedure for the election of its members would certainly strengthen the EP and should also make the MEPs known to their voters and, in turn, more responsible towards them[246]). The principle mentioned by the *European Constitutional Group* that the vote of each elector should be approximately equal to that of another[247]), seems to be widely agreed. The *Europäische Strukturkommission* advises the EP to take into account the impact of further widenings in its work organisation when drafting its proposal for a single European electoral procedure[248]). The *FT Round Table* even proposes an elaborated uniform electoral procedure[249]): it is proportional on the basis of regional lists but excludes national lists "which produce perfect proportionality but divorce MEPs from responsibility to individual constituents and give too much power to party machines"[250]). However, the proposal allows Britain to retain its single-member constituencies for the majority of British MEPs, while securing proportionality as in German national elections through supplementary national lists. A minority of MEPs could also be elected on the basis of European lists.

- An Austrian Perspective

On the one hand, Austria is one of the smaller countries in the EU and has a natural interest in keeping the present system of over-representation. On the other hand, there are at least two arguments suggesting the elaboration of a more sophisticated position. First, Austria is not the smallest Member state (at present there are five smaller ones) and will rank even higher in the event of further enlargements to the South and the East (in a Union of 28 there will be twelve smaller states than Austria and two others of almost the same size). Therefore, Austria's relative size drifts towards the middle and, consequently, it should think over its self-definition of being a 'small Member state': there are others which are over-represented even in relation to Austria.

---

246) *'Justus Lipsius'* 1995, 36.

247) European Constitutional Group 1993, 2c, p. 8.

248) Europäische Strukturkommission 1994, 38.

249) Federal Trust Papers N° 3, Annex 2.

250) Federal Trust Papers N° 3, 16.

The second argument relates to democratic and federal principles: so far, membership in the main institutions (for the Council see III.B.2.d.2, for the Commission III.B.2.c below) is biased in favour of the smaller states, although the functions of these institutions are quite different within the European polity. Over time, the Parliament's role gradually developed into that of a second (or first) legislative chamber on an almost equal footing with the Council, whose overriding importance diminished accordingly to that of a first (or second) chamber (see III.B.3.b.1 below). In contrast to the situation in the early days of European integration, Parliament is now directly elected; representatives of regional entities have the right to sit in the Council instead of national ministers[251]); and co-decision changed the role of the Commission considerably (see II.B.1). The institutional balance has changed and thus the respective roles of the institutions. Today, and probably increasingly after the next IGC, Council and Parliament are virtually two chambers of a quasi-federal system of governance in Europe. Over-representation of the smaller countries could be justified in terms of intergovernmentalism in the early days and can be in terms of the federal structure of the Union today. It conflicts nevertheless to some extent with democratic principles. In such a situation it seems advisable to apply the principle of proportionality and to restrict the deviation from the democratic ideal of 'one person one vote' to the necessary minimum.

Thus we suggest confining over-representation to the states' chamber (Council) and applying the principle of proportionality to the EP, with the single exception of a minimum number of three MEPs per state. This should secure an appropriate representation of the political spectrum of the smallest countries without distorting the proportionality principle too much[252]).

---

[251]) See Article 146 ECT.

[252]) A second necessity is to restrict the overall number of MEPs in order to keep the EP an efficient institution. The following could be a way to calculate the number of MEPs for each Member state: first, the exact proportion of the population of each Member state in comparison to the Union's population determines the number of MEPs according to a given size of Parliament (e.g. 700); in a second step the number of those countries which would not reach the minimum of three representatives will be increased accordingly. The necessary number of "additional" MEPs could either be added to the overall figure (i.e. 700 + x) or deducted from e.g. the larger Member states' contingents.

b) Major EC Appointments (including Judges) by the EP

In the early days of European integration, the appointment of the Commission (as well as of the members of other institutions like the Courts) was the exclusive right of the governments of the Member states, acting by common accord. The EP's impact was a rather theoretical one, as it could have forced any new Commission out of office via a motion of censure[253]) — a power which has never been used so far. With the single exception of consultation before appointments to the Court of Auditors [Article 206 (4) EECT, now 188b (3) ECT], only the Maastricht Treaty involved the European Parliament directly in the appointment process: now the Commission's President is nominated after consultation with the EP and, after the whole collegiate is nominated, it needs Parliament's assent (Article 158 ECT). Thus, the members of the new Santer Commission were the first to present themselves in individual hearings before an EP committee — a procedure which has been seen by the Council as possibly questioning the pre-existing institutional balance (see II.B.2). Furthermore, the TEU also provides for consultation of the EP when the President of the European Monetary Institute and later on the members of the Executive Board of the European System of Central Banks are chosen (Articles 109f and 109a ECT)[254]). However, even more far-reaching proposals are being debated at present concerning appointments within the European polity.

Some restrict their proposals to the first stage within the nomination of the Commission, i.e. the appointment of its President. The *FT Round Table* argues that the EP's power to approve the President of the Commission already exists in practice and should therefore be made explicit[255]). The *Europäische Strukturkommission* wants to see the Commission's President elected by the EP, which should also nominate the candidates. The result would have to be confirmed by the Council[256]). The members of the Commission should be chosen by the Commission's President and given assent by both the EP and the Council. Also the *European Parliament* itself wants to be granted the right to directly elect

---

[253]) Article 144 (2) ECT, see below.

[254]) In addition, the right of the EP to appoint the Ombudsperson (Article 138e ECT) could also be mentioned.

[255]) Federal Trust Papers N° 3, 21.

[256]) Europäische Strukturkommission 1994, 38.

the President of the Commission from among a list of names which should be established by the European Council[257]).

In addition, the *EP* claims the right to give its *assent* to *all* nominations to the Union's Courts (ECJ, CFI, and Court of Auditors), as well as to the members of the Executive Board of the European System of Central Banks[258]). The *Europäische Strukturkommission* is opposed to this idea: because matters of qualification and not political criteria should prevail, assent by the EP seems inappropriate to this group[259]). The *ECJ* itself argues that a hearing in the Parliament is unacceptable because the candidate might not be able to answer questions adequately without abandoning the necessary restraint of a personality whose independence — according to Article 168 (3) ECT — must be beyond doubt, and without anticipating his/her position in cases which s/he could possibly decide later[260]). In the so-called Donnelley working paper, however, MEPs already concluded that any such role for the EP should avoid purely political considerations, concentrating entirely on verifying whether a nominee could demonstrate his/her independence and outstanding legal qualifications or abilities[261]). '*Justus Lipsius*', on the other hand, voices doubts as to whether the direct and exclusive appointment by the governments should be prolonged. He mentions a suggestion by T. Koopmans that governments should nominate candidates and that an independent authority composed of the most senior members of the bench in each Member state should appoint the judges from the list of nominated candidates[262]).

---

[257]) EP Resolution from 17. 5. 1995, PE 190.441, pt. 21.iii.

[258]) EP Resolution from 17. 5. 1995, PE 190.441, pt. 23.ii; the idea had been previously launched by a working document on the composition and appointment of judicial organs and of the Court of Auditors prepared within the Institutional Affairs Committee by B. Donnelly, PE 211.536.

[259]) Europäische Strukturkommission 1994, 41.

[260]) ECJ Report from May 1995, pt. 17.

[261]) See PE 211.536.

[262]) '*Justus Lipsius*' 1995, 29.

Motion of Censure Against Single Commissioners

Article 144 ECT provides for the political complement to the investiture procedure[263]), i.e. the right of the EP to table a motion of censure against the Commission as a collegiate. If this is successful (a two-thirds majority representing a majority of MEPs is required), all Commissioners have to resign. However, the *EP* suggests that it (as well as the Council) should be able to request compulsory retirement of individual Commissioners, too — based on the argument that this be common to all national political systems[264]). This is also endorsed by the former French Prime Minister *Balladur* who wants to see dual Commission responsibility established before the European Council and the European Parliament[265]).

- An Austrian Perspective

Before developing any specific Austrian perspective, some structural reflections on the character and functions of the European Commission seem useful: While mostly being compared to a national government, the Commission is nonetheless significantly different both in terms of functions and legitimacy. As to the former, the main differences lie in the Commission's far-reaching monopoly of initiative and its powers to bring a legislative process to a halt by withdrawing its proposal. Neither is common in national systems (see also chapter III.B.2.f.1 concerning the de facto weakening of those powers at the EC level), despite the fact that national governments today clearly play an overriding role within the legislative agenda setting. On the other hand, the Commission is less powerful than a national government when it comes to implementing EC law (see chapter III.B.3.e on proposals to improve this weakness of the EC system). Despite all differences, an overall and comparative appreciation of the respective powers of the Commission and a Member state's government would suggest that both bodies have similarly prominent roles within their respective polities. Therefore, the Commission's legitimacy on the one hand, and the level of political control over it on the other, should not be less qualified than those of the national governments.

---

[263]) Interestingly, this parliamentary right is much older than the participation of the EP in the appointment of the Commission itself: the former was granted by the Merger Treaty in 1965, the latter only by the TEU in 1993.

[264]) EP Resolution from 17. 5. 1995, PE 190.441, pt. 21.iv.

[265]) Agence Europe, 2 December 1994, 1b.

Concerning the legitimacy of national governments, we are confronted with different models: the strongest certainly being the direct election of the head of government by the citizens, such as in the United States of America. In such a system, the government relies on a democratic legitimacy which is as direct as that of the parliament (respectively its first chamber). A somewhat more indirect legitimacy exists in those countries (like Austria) in which, after having been chosen by mainly the leader of the strongest party, the government depends on the good-will of the parliament. The old EEC procedure of having the Commission appointed by the Council — an institution composed of national governments which usually are only indirectly legitimated by the citizens — is clearly a step further away from direct legitimacy. The fact that the EP now participates in the process of appointing the Commission can be seen as a step in the direction of more legitimacy, similar to that which national parliaments enjoy. The assent by both the Council and EP brings in one directly and one indirectly legitimated institution — a model that seems well adapted to the specific structure of the Union. The logical next step in that development would be to give Parliament the right to elect the Commission President (and not only to give its assent to a decision taken by the Member states' governments). Although, in order to safeguard the necessary balance between the federal and the democratic principle, Parliament might be bound to an extensive list of candidates established by the Council. It seems furthermore recommendable in terms of coherence and practical working capacity that the appointed President of the Commission chooses his/her team, again from a list put forward by the Council. The whole Commission would then be subject to hearings and a final vote in Parliament — something which has already proved to be a convincing procedure.

However, not only the terms of investiture constitute the (formal) democratic legitimacy of a body. The conditions and procedures for termination of that office are crucial, too. Here, we witness still a significant difference to the national levels, where usually the parliaments as well as the head of government may withdraw individual members of government. At the EU level, the Council has no power to call back the Commission or any single member of it, while the EP may only vote a motion of censure on the collegiate as a whole. The fact that the EP has developed into an important actor with direct legitimacy from the citizens, suggests that time might have come to allow for a more efficient political control of the Commissioners during their five year term in office. The Commission's fields of activity have been considerably extended parallel to the increase of the Union's powers and — unlike the original High Authority of the ECSC-Treaty, which mainly carried out what was written in the Treaty or decided by the Council of Ministers — it is an active policy-making institution. In support of our point, we could argue in addition that increased political control by the EP would help to consolidate the independence of the Commission which was designed by the founding fathers of the Community as an institution independent from purely national interests and thus counter-balancing the Council.

Looking at the considerable powers given to the Commission, it seems to be in the interests of the Austrian citizens and politicians to improve both political control over this body and its legitimacy. Strengthening the "checks and balances" within the EC system should be one of the leitmotifs of the forthcoming IGC. Therefore, the same argument is valid for appointments to the other EC institutions such as the Courts and the European Central Bank. We cannot see any reason why members of government should be better equipped than members of parliament to judge the abilities of for example a judge. This is not a purely normative consideration in terms of democratic theory, but also relies on practical reasons: up to now, the representatives of the Member states in the Council have not had any opportunity to assess the abilities for example of the candidates put forward by the other Member states (it would not be feasible for every Member state government to organise a hearing with all candidates). Therefore, their decision to join the necessary 'common accord' relies on purely tactical considerations. Only by a public hearing (and who is better equipped to organise such an event than a parliamentary body?) can the necessary information be revealed and made the basis of a sound judgement and decision.

In Austria, it is beyond doubt that the Parliament is a prime actor when it comes to the appointment of comparable offices (auditors, supreme judges). Therefore, the directly elected representatives of the European citizens should be at least on an equal footing with the Council when it comes to major appointments in the Union. The most convincing model seems to be to give the Council the right to propose an extensive list of candidates, and Parliament the power to choose from it. Concerning the ECJ, the list of candidates should ideally be established by a body composed of the most senior members of the bench in each Member state.

c) Number of Commissioners

With a view to further enlargements of the Union, the issue of increasing numbers of Commissioners has also been put on the agenda. While the Commission itself does not address this matter[266]), the Council hesitates to judge whether the number of twenty Commissioners is "excessive with a view to secure the greatest possible efficiency of the Commission" because it is, after only a few months, "still too early"[267]). However, the European Council meeting in Corfu on 24/25 June 1994 put the issue on the agenda of the forthcoming IGC[268]).

Some argue that the size of the collegiate of Commissions should be reduced in order to make it more efficient. When setting out France's guidelines for institutional reforms, the French Prime Minister *Balladur* called it a necessity "to reduce the number of Commissioners if one wants the Commission to remain, as would be desirable, a collegial body for efficient and rapid decision-making."[269]) The President of the National Assembly in France, *Seguin*, elaborated a more detailed proposal suggesting that "once the Commission has been clearly redirected to its administrative role, there is nothing to prevent a reduction in Commissioners, either so that each country only appoints one Commissioner, or that the large countries, if they chair the European Council in turn, do not, in exchange, appoint a Commissioner"[270]). The quite surprising equation of Commissioners, on the one hand, and Council presidency, on the other, was also suggested by the French Senate: Its *Guéna Report* links the introduction of team Presidencies with reducing the number of Commissioners of the larger states from two to one, in order to counterbalance the loss of influence of the smaller states in the Council[271]).

Most contributions, however, tackle the number of Commissioners as a question per se. In the *Parliament's* view there should continue to be at least

---

266) Cf. its chapter on "The Commission" in Commission Report, SEC(95) 731, 11 f.

267) Council document SN 1821/95, pt. 31.

268) Pt. IV of the conclusions of the Presidency, published e.g. as Annex Ia) to Council document SN 1823/95.

269) Agence Europe, 2 December 1994, 1b.

270) Quotation from Agence Europe, 8 December 1994, 5.

271) Guéna Report (French Senate) 1995, 19.

one Commissioner per Member state[272]). *Agence Europe* put forward the idea of having one Commissioner from each larger country and some Commissioners from the smaller Member states on a rotating basis[273]). The *FT Round Table* argues that reducing the smaller Member states' number of Commissioners would not be acceptable for them and would alienate those citizens without a national in the Commission. Therefore, it proposes a maximum of one Commissioner per Member state, but the President and six Vice-Presidents could comprise a form of inner cabinet[274]). In his speech on the future of integration on 22 May 1995[275]), the Irish Foreign Minister *Dick Spring* claims that the right to nominate a Commissioner is essential, but each country should have only one.

Others want to completely abolish the nationality criterion: for example the *Europäische Strukturkommission* proposes that the Commission should be composed according to the needs of the departmental divisions of the Commission (in German: 'Ressortprinzip') without national quota, and that its number be reduced rather than increased[276]). This is also an alternative acceptable to *'Justus Lipsius'* who suggests that the designated Commission President choose the 14 other members ("one for every 40 million inhabitants or so, the biggest countries being limited to one member only") according to their capacities and not their nationality[277]). Nonetheless, a fundamental argument forwarded by *'Lipsius'* should not be disregarded: is it not "a little surprising when one realises that most governments of the Member states count 30, 40 or even more members and that the Commission is able to take all its decisions by a simple majority, which is a guarantee of a good functioning"[278])?

- An Austrian Perspective

Looking at the recent past of Austrian integration in the European Union, we think that the existence of an Austrian Commissioner did indeed matter,

---

[272]) EP Resolution from 17. 5. 1995, PE 190.441, pt. 21.ii.

[273]) Agence Europe, 2 December 1994, 1b.

[274]) Federal Trust Papers N° 3, 22.

[275]) See Agence Europe, 24 May 1995, 3f.

[276]) Europäische Strukturkommission 1994, 41.

[277]) *'Justus Lipsius'* 1995, 28.

[278]) *'Justus Lipsius'* 1995, 27.

both in terms of bringing European politics closer to Austrian politicians and citizens, and in terms of making Austrian administrative traditions (and sometimes even political positions) known at the supranational level. Clearly, the representation of national interests is essentially enshrined in the Council, and the equilibrium between democratic representation, on the one hand, and national representation, on the other, has to be arranged via the distribution of powers between the Council of Ministers and the European Parliament. It is not evident why countries with larger population should have more members in the collegiate of Commissioners, while it seems perfectly reasonable that all countries have an interest in representation of their specific bureaucratic culture in the Commission at the highest level (and the same is true for the legal traditions which should be represented in the EC Courts).

As mentioned above, it is by no means evident that a collegiate of, say, 28 Commissioners should not be capable of working effectively. Clearly, this will also depend on the internal structure of this body (e.g., a stronger principle of political leadership might be introduced via reinforcing the President of the Commission, or via distinguishing between junior and senior Commissioners). Many questions raised here do, in fact, less concern the democratic character of the Union than models of administrative organisation (which cannot be discussed here in detail).

From the Austrian viewpoint, one Commissioner for all Member states will clearly be the preferred option. If it should prove desirable to decrease numbers in the long term, it seems important to at least stipulate that no country be excluded from having a Commissioner for too long a period, for example not longer than one term of office (five years).

The idea of letting the Commission President choose his collaborators according to their qualifications is an interesting one (see III.B.2.b above). However, it does not answer the question of whether each country should have a national within the collegiate, as clearly no Member state is too small to be capable of proposing adequate nationals as candidates for all possible posts.

d) Presidency of the Council

At present the Presidency of the Council is occupied by each Member state in turn, for six months at a time. This rotation principle helps to integrate each state in the Union system. The establishment of the so-called Troika, i.e. the closer co-operation between the previous, the present and the next Presidency[279]), has contributed to more coherence of the Council's work. However, there are still "serious defects: the very long time, already over seven years, before a Member state's turn comes round again; the interruption of business due to changes in priorities as between Presidencies; and the variable capacity to deal with problems of foreign and security policy in particular."[280]) The problem of long intervals and the varying capacity of the different Member states to cope with the demanding tasks of Presidency will be even more apparent in the event of further enlargements. Therefore, several contributions have been made with a view to reorganising the Council's structure. They relate to the term in office of the Presidencies (i.), to the composition of the Presidency itself (ii.), to the abolishment of the automatism of change in Presidencies (iii.), and to the introduction of different presidencies for the various Council formations (iv.).

(i.) Concerning the problem of non-coherence of the work of the Council due to the frequent changes of the Presidency, for example the later French President *Chirac* made the suggestion to "lengthen the period of Presidency in order to benefit from the indispensable duration of any far-reaching action, with the addition of two Vice-presidencies"[281]). The French Minister of European Affairs, *Lamassoure*, suggested that the Presidency should last "three, four, five years"[282]). The *Europäische Strukturkommission* proposes a period of at least one year[283]). In this respect *'Justus Lipsius'* considers that a one year duration would involve only a small improvement in the external representation of the EU and, on the other hand, would lead to very long intervals for each country[284]).

(ii.) Since a change in the term of office does not solve the other problems mentioned above, another idea would be to strengthen the role of the other members of the Troika and simultaneously change the order so that at least one major Member state is part of every Troika. For instance, the *Europäische Strukturkommission* wants to see the modus of Troika practised with prolonged

---

[279]) See Article J.5 (3) TEU.

[280]) Federal Trust Papers N° 3, 9.

[281]) Cited from Agence Europe, 23 March 1995, 2.

[282]) Cited from Agence Europe, 1 February 1995, 2.

[283]) Europäische Strukturkommission 1994, 37.

[284]) *'Justus Lipsius'* 1995, 21.

terms of office, always including two smaller and one big Member state[285]). The *FT Round Table* wants to stay with the present system but proposes an adaptation of the division of labour between the members of the Troika to the differing requirements of the Community and the CFSP: "For Community matters, the Presidency of the Council is eased by the role of the Commission in maintaining coherence and initiative in the Community's programme and in conducting its external negotiations. The chairing of the different functional Councils (...) could be shared out among the different members of the Troika. For the foreign and security policy, however, the Commission's role is weaker and the capacity of the larger Member states is relatively more significant. So there would be merit in arranging the Troikas so that each contains one of them, which in this field would be *primus inter pares*."[286])

Improving the Troika system essentially remains on secure ground as there would be a single Presidency with the other members of the Troika only performing auxiliary tasks. While sticking to the idea of involving more states in the Presidency, some go further and conceive abolition of the principle of a single state leading the Union. *Ludlow/Ersbøll* propose *'team Presidencies'*, "in which Member states in a larger Union might be divided into four or five groups, each representing approximately 100 million citizens. Each group could then exercise the Presidency of the Union for a year or eighteen months, ensuring that everybody had a lengthy term at least every six years. Ideally, the groups should reflect different characteristics and interests: west and east, north and south."[287]) They argue that this would enhance the legitimacy of the Presidency, would facilitate specialisation, and reduce the adverse effects of variable quality. The *Guéna Report* amends this proposal by suggesting that the big state that is leading the team should be the President of the European Council and of those Councils with reference to the Union's international relations, whereas the assisting smaller states could be in charge of the other specialised Councils[288]).

(iii.) Another prominent idea would be to abolish the rigid rules for a change in Presidency every six months (or whatever the period might be) and to replace it by some sort of election. The *Europäische Strukturkommission*

---

[285]) Europäische Strukturkommission 1994, 37.

[286]) Federal Trust Papers N° 3, 9 (emphasis in the original).

[287]) *Ludlow/Ersbøll* (CEPS) 1995, 40.

[288]) Guéna Report (French Senate) 1995, 17.

wants to see political leadership increased by an elected Council Presidency for the period of at least one year[289]). It is also thought that the election would increase legitimacy and cohesion of the Council. According to the proposed Constitution of the *Herman Report,* the President of the Council should be elected by an (unweighted) majority of five sixths of the Member states for a period of one year. The mandate could be extended up to three years[290]). *'Justus Lipsius''* proposal for a separate CFSP Presidency is also based on an election in the Council[291]).

Ludlow/Ersbøll propose a vote of no confidence in the Presidency by Parliament arguing that, alone, the possibility would introduce a new edge into relations between Parliament and Council, "to the benefit of both"[292]). A vote of no confidence should have "consequences that could in certain circumstances necessitate the resignation of the Presidency in question"[293]).

(iv.) *'Justus Lipsius'* reports the idea of splitting the Presidency of the Council: there could be different Presidencies; each of them being elected for and by each different formation of the Council for a given period of several years[294]). However, this proposal seems to endanger the very aim of increased consistency because "conducting a Presidency means ensuring consistency between the various formations of the Council, as well as the co-ordination of hundreds of meetings and the necessity of deciding to give priorities to some of them"[295]). To overcome this criticism a slightly different proposal would be to separate the CFSP role from the other functions of the Presidency: the Council would elect a long-term Presidency, but only for the European and General Affairs Councils[296]). Another suggestion from the French Minister of Foreign Affairs, *Lamassoure*, was that "there should be as many presidencies as Councils of Ministers"[297]).

---

[289]) Europäische Strukturkommission 1994, 37.

[290]) Herman Report 1994, Article 19 of the proposed Constitution.

[291]) *'Justus Lipsius'* 1995, 22.

[292]) *Ludlow/Ersbøll* (CEPS) 1995, 48.

[293]) *Ludlow/Ersbøll* (CEPS) 1995, 39.

[294]) *'Justus Lipsius'* 1995, 22.

[295]) *'Justus Lipsius'* 1995, 22.

[296]) *'Justus Lipsius'* 1995, 22 f.

[297]) Cited from Agence Europe, 1 February 1995, 2.

(1) Union President

At present, the Presidency of the Council is also the Presidency of the European Union, since it represents the Union [Art J.5 (1) TEU]. With a view to enhancing the Union's legitimacy in the eyes of its citizens, however, there have been proposals to change this system radically and to unlink Council Presidency from Union Presidency.

The later French President *Chirac* suggested establishing "a President of the European Union who would be appointed by the EU for three years"[298]). The main task of this President should be to represent the Union externally and to ensure that its interests are defended and its identity promoted. In contrast, the French Minister for European Affairs, *Lamassoure*, rejects the idea of a Union Presidency because there is no room for two presidential positions in the system [what role would this President play in relation to the European Commission?"[299])].

The *European Constitutional Group*'s constitution provides for a "President of the Union" to be elected by the Chamber of Parliamentarians of the Member states from their membership[300]). This President should only exert representative functions, like granting pardons for offences against the laws of the Union, and receiving foreign ambassadors; but s/he might also, on extra-ordinary occasions, convene the Parliamentarian bodies in joint session.

(2) Composition of the Council

Another series of proposals in order to make the Council more coherent have been put forward relating to the composition of the Member states' delegations. The *FT Round Table* reiterates the old idea of a proper Minister for European Affairs with the rank of Minister of State. Since the original idea was not workable in view of the division of competencies within national governments, the Round Table does not want to see the European Affairs Minister representing his/her country in all Councils, but only participating in each state's delegation to all Councils (led by the specific departmental minister), thus facilitating co-ordination at the political level[301]). In contrast, the *Herman*

---

[298]) Cited from Agence Europe, 23 March 1995, 2.

[299]) Agence Europe, 1 February 1995, 2.

[300]) European Constitutional Group 1993, Article V of the proposed constitution.

[301]) Federal Trust Papers N° 3, 10.

Report, which also proposes that the Council members should be ministers charged with European affairs, suggests that the delegation should be led by this special minister according to national provisions[302]). The French President of the National Assembly, *Seguin,* proposes that the Permanent representative, "pivot of the system and guarantor of its coherence, should be a minister" sitting in all Councils, possibly along with the relevant technical minister[303]). Former French President *Mitterand* and Germany's Chancellor *Kohl* proposed, in November 1993, the establishment of an intermediate body composed of Ministers for European Affairs, who should be present in Brussels on a semi-permanent basis[304]).

Departing from the present system, the French Minister for European Affairs, *Lamassoure,* suggested that governments could be invited to incorporate one or more members of their parliaments into the delegations that attend meetings of the Council. The former President of the EP, *Hänsch,* is strongly opposed to this idea: "This seems to me as inappropriate, Member states are represented by governments as the Union is a Union of Member states"[305]).

● An Austrian Perspective

The prestigious job of the **Presidency of the Council** is one of the rare opportunities for smaller countries to play a noteworthy role in the international context that is usually dominated by the much larger countries. Losing this opportunity, as proposed by some, is therefore not attractive from the Austrian perspective.

Although it has to be acknowledged that Parliament's position has been strengthened considerably, the Council still plays a pivotal role in the decision-making of the Union. Past experience has shown that the dynamics of the Community/Union depend heavily on the efficiency of the Council Presidency. From this perspective, reaching the aims of securing coherence of the Council's work and of adequate external leadership has to be part of a satisfactory solution. But these goals have to be balanced against the understandable wish of the smaller Member states to play a significant role. Any solution which

---

[302]) Herman Report 1994, Article 17 of the proposed Constitution.

[303]) Agence Europe, 8 December 1994, 5.

[304]) See *'Justus Lipsius'* 1995, 31.

[305]) *Hänsch* 1995, 6.

excludes a group of states would conflict with the Council's function as a states' chamber. However, not every shift in the balance will lead automatically to opposition of the smaller states since they are well aware of the natural imbalance of resources.

Within the many proposals made in this respect, four main ideas have emerged: the principle of team Presidencies; the system of elected Presidencies; the principle of rotation; and the extension of the term of office. If combined elaborately, they may add up to a consensus-oriented system which meets all three requirements (coherence, leadership, and participation of all Member states). Thus, three groups of five states could be formed: the group of the largest states (at present: Germany, France, Great Britain, Italy, and Spain); the group of the medium sized states (at present: Belgium, Greece, Netherlands, Portugal, and Sweden); and the group of smaller states (at present: Denmark, Ireland, Luxembourg, Finland, and Austria). In the event of enlargement, it might be necessary to build a fourth or even fifth group in order to secure balanced groups of approximately equal size. The groups, every eighteen months, elect one Member state which then becomes a member of the team Presidency. The three (or four, or five) members of the team distribute the 'portfolios', i.e. the leading responsibility and therefore the chairmanship in the individual Councils, among them by common accord. It is understood that the external representation is performed by this innovative Troika, normally under the leadership of the delegated member of the first group.

Our proposed model solves a number of the problems addressed above: First, the small Member states are not excluded from external representation, although one of those states best equipped to represent the Union is always part of the team. Second, since the Presidency is carried out by a team with overall responsibility for the whole of the Council's activities (the distribution of 'portfolios' only being a technical or co-ordinating type of 'leadership') and stays in office for a longer period, overall coherence is facilitated. Third, the principle of strict rotation (among the group members) is replaced by an internal election. Membership in the team Presidency will rotate among all members of the group as a rule because of the traditional political climate which has been consensus-oriented and co-operative. However, the election provides an opportunity to make the sequence more flexible: if a state is in deep political crisis, if its internal constitutional rules provide for a general election with a chance of a change in government, or if it has a weak minority government at the time of election, it would not be a good idea to burden this Member state with the demanding task of Presidency. In fact, there should even be a provision for a by-election if such developments unexpectedly disturb a term of Presidency. Finally, it does not, per se, extend the time each state has to wait for its turn of Presidency (although the term of office could be extended up to the proposed time of eighteen months).

A **separate Union President** not linked to the Council would be a remarkable step from the quasi-federal and sui-generis-type model of the Union towards a more classical state-like model. Apart from the obvious objection that this would not be a consensual model, it is questionable what function a separate Union Presidency could have. First, a purely symbolic function such as for example that which the Heads of State and monarchs in some Member states perform, would not be very successful because it is hardly imaginable that even an outstanding personality of a single Member state could be of comparable appeal for the rest of the Union's citizens. In this respect the situation is completely different from any nation state, even of the size of the USA, where differences of culture, language, or tradition do not play an equally important role. Second, this individual person could hardly represent the Union in its external relations. The negative example of the rivalry between the Austrian government and its present Federal President illustrates the likely difficulties and problems raised by such an institution: all the competencies as regards the content of external policy are vested in the Austrian Parliament and the Federal Government, whereas the Federal President has no specific resources and competencies apart from the specific function of formal external representation of the country. Third, any co-ordinating function with respect to the Council of Ministers would be equally misplaced because a single person without an additional apparatus could not be of any help. Furthermore, such a President would alter the institutional balance considerably. If it turns out that despite our arguments a need for a purely symbolic President should emerge, we would advocate attaching this function to the President of the European Parliament, as is the case in Austria if the elected Federal President should die while holding office.

As to the **composition of the Council,** even the relatively short Austrian experience with European affairs reveals an overriding need for internal co-ordination among the different ministries. The idea of consistently delegating from each Member state both the respective specialised minister, and the Minister for European Affairs in charge of internal co-ordination, seems to meet both requirements: internal co-ordination of the national representatives in the

Council and improved co-ordination and coherence between the different functional Councils. The idea could be supported by a co-ordinated working schedule providing for Council meetings only in the second half of the week. This would give the Minister for European Affairs the opportunity to be at the seat of her/his government for the rest of the week to fulfil the internal co-ordinating function.

e) The Future of the Committee of the Regions

The CoR started its work only recently. So far, its experience only includes the procedure of appointing members of the Committee, and the drafting of a couple of opinions. Therefore, the few proposals made with respect to it concern mainly its composition: the *EP* wants members of the CoR to be elected members of a local or regional assembly[306]). The *Herman Report*[307]) and the CoR itself[308]) also endorse this idea.

Some, such as the *German Bundestag*[309]) and the CoR itself[310]), ask for reinforcement of the position of the Committee of the Regions, which should for example obtain the right to file lawsuits with the EU Court of Justice. Parliament[311]), as well as the CoR[312]), want the EP to be able to consult the Committee (as well as the ESC) on the same footing as the Council and the Commission. The *FT Round Table* calls for giving the CoR its own budget and secretariat. The CoR should be treated as an "important advisory body" but should not be transformed into a third (legislative) chamber because -"it is not desirable to complicate the legislative process yet further"[313]). The CoR also calls for institutional independence[314]).

The *EP* wants to strengthen the CoR's role of drawing up policies in order to improve the economic and social cohesion and to respect the principle of

---

306) EP Resolution from 17. 5. 1995, PE 190.441, pt. 27.

307) Herman Report 1994, Article 29 of the proposed Constitution.

308) CoR Resolution from 20 April 1995, CdR 136/95, pt. 5.

309) Agence Europe, 1 April 1995, 3.

310) CoR Resolution from 20 April 1995, CdR 136/95, pt. 2 f.

311) EP Resolution from 17. 5. 1995, PE 190.441, pt. 27.

312) CoR Resolution from 20 April 1995, CdR 136/95, pt. 8.

313) Federal Trust Papers N° 3, 28.

314) CoR Resolution from 20 April 1995, CdR 136/95, pt. 4 ff.

subsidiarity[315]). The most radical proposal comes from the *European Constitutional Group* which suggests veto powers for the CoR in all cases where Community action "would infringe upon the powers of regional or local authorities on the Member states. Any such proposals must be adopted by a two thirds majority of the Committee"[316]). The *Committee of the Regions* itself wants to increase the cases where an opinion by it be obligatory and that the Union legislator be required to give the reasons in cases where it does not follow the CoR's opinion[317]).

- ● An Austrian Perspective

Austria is a federal state composed of nine *'Länder'* with autonomy and important competencies. Their room of manoeuvre might be smaller than that of the German 'Länder', but it is much larger than that of for example French 'départements'. The Austrian 'Länder' had to give up some of their traditional competencies in favour of the supranational EC-level. The negotiations between the 'Bund' and the 'Länder' with a view to compensating the loss of competencies have not been brought to an end, although the assent of the 'Länder' to the EU-adhesion (via the 'Bundesrat', the second chamber of Parliament) was originally bound to a positive result in this respect. However, the participation of the 'Länder' in European affairs is laid down in a new section on European Union in the Austrian Constitution (Article 23d B-VG): if there is a uniform opinion of the 'Länder', the Austrian (federal) representative in the EU Council is bound by it unless "compelling arguments in the field of foreign or integration policy" force the 'Bund' to depart from the opinion. Therefore, the regional interests are being 'digested' and 'mediated' through a specific national channelling procedure.

Against this background, up-grading the Committee of the Regions at the supranational level seems undesirable, be it via, either, granting it the right to be consulted in virtually all Union matters, or even the right to veto legislation. But what is more, both options would lead eventually to a situation where the CoR could be called a third legislative chamber of the Union. Considering that the quasi-federal structure of the Union is already a very complicated and deli-

---

[315]) EP Resolution from 17. 5. 1995, PE 190.441, pt. 28.

[316]) European Constitutional Group 1993, 2c, p. 7.

[317]) CoR Resolution from 20 April 1995, CdR 136/95, pt. 8.

cate construction, and that the decision-making by a two-chamber system is already a lengthy process susceptible to deadlocks, a third chamber would not seem advisable.

Looking at the considerable differences in size, organisation and competencies of the various 'regions' represented in the CoR, the idea of a third chamber seems to contradict even the very principle of subsidiarity! Why should the Union enhance the powers of a French 'département' by giving it a voice at the European level when France decides to stay a very centralised state? In fact, not interfering in the internal structure of political representation and thus preserving cultural as well as political diversity has often been seen as a guiding principle of the Union's structure. Therefore, representation of regional interests should be channelled internally by the governments and mediated by their representatives in the Council. Those regions or 'Länder' which have more competencies and autonomy could, (and already do), in addition take the opportunity to set up their own representations in Brussels and use the lobbying channels open to everyone.

Considering the experience of the Economic and Social Committee and its similar diversity in membership, it is not to be expected that the CoR will have the capacity to make valuable contributions to the policy process without enhancing its facilities and resources considerably. But even if this expensive precondition was fulfilled, the reported diversity of the different regional entities represented in the Committee challenges not only this body's coherence (and that of its opinions), but also its position vis-à-vis the other chambers of the Union, notably the Council. While the representatives of German or Austrian 'Länder' may be used to oppose their federal government even in questions of general policies, this might be structurally inappropriate against the background of the national position of the French delegation to the CoR. Furthermore, regional differences and diversity of regional interests are already at the very heart of the differences between Member states' positions in the Council. Also for those reasons, the national level seems to be most appropriate for building up a wider regional consensus. Introducing the possibility that a representative of a region could be the national representative at ministerial level in the Council of Ministers (new Article 146 ECT) is an important step in acknowledging this specific role of the national governments.

f) The Relationship Between the EU System and National Parliaments

In this chapter, we will first provide an historical overview and then outline the prevailing differences between the national systems of parliamentary involvement in European affairs. Subsequently, the relevant proposals and counterproposals shall be presented, followed — as usual — by some comments from the Austrian viewpoint.

(1) Historical Development and National Models

Notwithstanding the common belief that relations between national parliaments and the EP are a new topic within the debate of reforming democracy at the European level, there is a substantial past to build on[318]). Originally, there was the closest possible connection between the two levels of parliamentary scrutiny as the Members of European Parliament were drawn from the parliaments of the Member states, which obviously provided good grounding for intense communication between the parliamentary bodies. However, there was the major disadvantage that members' attention and working capacity was split between the two centres of activity[319]). This was the major reason why with the first direct elections of the EP in 1979, the number of dual mandates in the national and European Parliaments dropped substantially to around 30 (despite the fact that the 1976 Act on direct EP elections still allowed for it). During the first period of the directly elected EP, contacts to national parliaments accordingly decreased.

However, joint meetings by the Presidents of national parliaments and the European Parliament were held each second year from 1983. After the 1989 European elections, relations with national parliaments were strengthened by the establishment of the Conference of Community affairs bodies of the Parliaments of the European Union (*COSAC*). At least twice a year since, delegations of national and European MPs have met to debate specific matters of common interest. The meetings used to be prepared on the basis of a questionnaire sent by the organising parliament in order to broaden available information and focus the debate. More recently, this body has also provided for debates with the Ministers of the country presiding over the Council of Ministers;

---

[318]) This passage draws particularly on *Hänsch* 1995.

[319]) A shortcoming that would have weighted even heavier at later times when the EP saw its work load substantially increased after the Single European Act.

thus offering a unique opportunity to many national representatives. The number of such meetings increased substantially (to 25 between 1991-1994), as did the number of bilateral meetings between specific rapporteurs or committees[320]). Recently, national parliaments have also increasingly called on MEPs (usually from their own country) to give evidence to them.

Within the preparation of the Maastricht IGC, the first *conference of parliaments* (or *assizes*) was held in November 1990, designed to influence the negotiations on the new Treaty. This conference, attended by over 300 parliamentarians (one third MEPs), adopted a resolution calling on the IGC to take account of the specific proposals of the EP. It also asked for enhanced "co-operation between the national parliaments and the EP, through regular meetings of specialised committees, exchanges of information and by organising conferences of parliaments of the EC when the discussion of guidelines of vital importance to the Community justifies it, in particular when intergovernmental conferences are being held"[321]).

This suggestion was followed by the governments who adopted two *Common Declarations*, N° 13 and 14, annexed to the Final Act of the Maastricht Treaty, dealing with the role of the national parliaments and the assizes respectively. The first recognises the importance of encouraging "greater involvement of national parliaments in the activities of the European Union", calling for contacts between national parliaments and their European counterpart to be improved. It also emphasises the commitment of the national governments to transmit to their parliaments in good time Commission proposals for EC legislation. The second Common Declaration invites the EP and the national parliaments to meet "as necessary" as *assizes*. This conference shall be consulted on the main features of the Union, and the Presidents of both the Council and the Commission will report on the state of the Union on any such occasion. Concerning other provisions of the Treaties, a role for national parliaments is implicitly envisaged under the following headings: Article N and O TEU on amendments to the Treaty and on the accession of new Member states respectively provide for ratification according to national constitutional rules. Approval of acts by national parliaments via the "national constitutional rules" is referred to in connection with conventions and the "communautarisation" of

---

[320]) The Commission Report gives the number of 44 meetings between different bodies belonging to national and European parliaments in 1993, see SEC(95) 731, 16.

[321]) Quoted from *Hänsch* 1995, 2.

action in certain areas in the field of JHA (Articles K 3 (2c) and K 9), with additions to citizens' rights (Article 8e ECT), the uniform procedure for election of MEPs (Article 138(3) ECT), the decision on own resources (Article 201 ECT), and the ratification of conventions according to Article 220 ECT[322]). Clearly, the parliaments are also usually prominently involved in the transposition of EC Directives into national law (Article 189 ECT).

However, parliamentary scrutiny over EC affairs has always differed significantly within the national political systems in Europe. While some national parliaments focus on the debate of broad outlines of European policy, others (in the first place, the Danish) try to monitor legislative activity at the EC-level and specifically the voting behaviour of their governments within the Council, in more detail. Since the adoption of the Maastricht Treaty, we have witnessed a tendency to increase the role of national parliaments in several Member states. For example, the French constitution was amended to include a new Article permitting the National Assembly and the Senate to adopt resolutions on all proposals for Community acts containing provisions of a legislative nature. Both houses seem to have put considerable pressure on the government to conform with their resolutions[323]). However, proposals under the CFSP as well as JHA (second and third pillar) are still not made available there. In Germany, too, the constitution was amended. Furthermore, transfers of competencies to the European level will need two-thirds majorities in both parliamentary chambers. In addition, the German government was obliged to inform Bundestag and Bundesrat comprehensively on EC matters, and at the earliest opportunity. Within the new Member states (especially Austria) there is also a trend to give the parliaments comparatively far-reaching powers to control their governments' Euro-actions.

(2) Reform Proposals

Up to now, we have witnessed the development of an increasingly dense net of communication between national and European parliaments, and a tendency to increase the national parliaments' attention to the single governments' European policies. Yet, there has so far been little or no debate on any direct legislative role for national parliaments at the European level. Such ideas have only recently been thrown into the reform debates preceding the forthcoming IGC

---

[322]) See Commission Report, SEC(95) 731, 17.

[323]) See *Hänsch* 1995, 3.

by mainly the French polity. In its so-called *Guéna Report,* the French Senate seeks to enhance democratic legitimacy of the Union almost exclusively by giving the national parliaments competencies at the Euro-level. Thus, representatives of the national parliaments sitting in a 'European Senate' should play a crucial role in questions of subsidiarity and in the intergovernmental pillars[324]). Guéna also suggests that representatives of national parliaments participate in the formation of some Council delegations, and that all inter-institutional agreements be submitted to a simplified ratification procedure in the national parliaments[325]). To better enable national parliaments to follow European policy debates, he calls for quicker transmission of Commission proposals. Other French politicians have also promoted the idea of involving the national parliaments in EC decision-making, including Prime Ministers *Edouard Balladur*[326]) and *Alain Juppé*[327]). President *Jacques Chirac* expressed his hope "that national parliaments may be involved in the process for developing Union standards"[328]), and the Minister for European Affairs, *Lamassoure,* desires that national parliamentarians be allowed representation "when the Council legislates"[329]). The President of the French National Assembly, *Seguin,* suggested that "national parliaments collectively play the role of the lower house, and the European Parliament that of the upper chamber"[330]).

Apart from French politicians, the *British* also tend to stress the role of the national parliaments for the legitimacy of the EC polity — first of all their Prime Minister *John Major.*

> "The EP sees itself as the future democratic focus for the Union. But this is a flawed ambition, because the European Union is an association of States, deriving its basic democratic legitimacy through *national parliaments*. That should remain the case (...) It is national

---

[324]) Guéna Report (French Senate) 1995, 14 and 39 f.

[325]) Guéna Report (French Senate) 1995, 24 ff.

[326]) Le Monde 30 November 1994; see also *'Justus Lipsius'* 1995, 37.

[327]) See Agence Europe, 25 May 1995, 2.

[328]) Cited from Agence Europe, 23 March 1995, 2b.

[329]) Agence Europe, 1 February 1995, 3.

[330]) Agence Europe, 8 December 1994, 5.

parliamentary democracy that confers legitimacy on the European Council"[331]).

While the powers of the EP should not be strengthened in the coming IGC, *Major* believes that

> "much more should be done to build links between national parliaments and the European Parliament (...) We all need to develop a more co-operative effort with the EP and we must examine how this can be done. In my own country, I see a case for Joint Committees (both by inviting MEPs to contribute to national scrutiny committees, and vice versa)"[332]).

Thus, the British want to see the role of the national parliaments enhanced, but seem not to go as far as suggesting a direct role for national parliaments at the European level, for example via a second parliamentary chamber[333]). On the other hand, the legitimacy of the directly elected EP is challenged to an even higher extent than by the French. For example, there was a noteworthy dispute between the British representative in the Reflection Group on the IGC, *David Davis* (known as "Euro-sceptic"), and the British Vice-President of the EP and co-rapporteur on the IGC, *David Martin*, on the role of national parliaments vis-à-vis the European counterpart. While Davis reproached powers being removed "from national parliaments which have democratic legitimacy and (...) [given] to the European Parliament"[334]) (implying that the latter would not have any), Martin countered that the EP

> "is not seeking to take further powers from national parliaments but to have the ability to scrutinise those powers that national parliaments have *already* ceded to the European Union's Council of Ministers and to the Commission. It is in these areas that national parliamentary scrutiny, which is at best only partial, must be complemented by the detailed scrutiny brought by the EP whose mem-

---

[331]) *John Major*, Speech at the University of Leiden, 7 September 1994, p. 8 of manuscript (emphasis in original).

[332]) *John Major*, Speech at the University of Leiden, 7 September 1994, p. 9 of manuscript.

[333]) However, the British EC-Commissioner *Leon Brittan* has obviously suggested that such an institution, called "Chamber of Subsidiarity", be introduced (see *Hänsch* 1995, 6).

[334]) Frankfurter Allgemeine Zeitung, 17 January 1995; English quotation from Agence Europe, 26 January 1995, 2.

bers are, after all, chosen to deal specifically with such European issues."[335])

Like David Martin, many commentators and politicians have stressed that a systematic division of tasks is necessary between the national parliaments and the EP. For example, *Jacques Delors* argued that a second parliamentary chamber consisting of national parliamentarians would confuse European citizens with regard to the tasks of either group:

> "Either a national parliament decides, for reasons of apparent national interest, to transfer part of the exercise of sovereignty to the Union. In that case, who is responsible before it once it has solemnly agreed to this transfer of sovereignty? It is the government which represents the Member state at the Union level. Or else the matter remains a national competence and we remain in the national rules and things are clear. But if a parliament asks to play a role in the preparation of decisions transferred to the Union, then I say that it will be a mess. In such a case, we are going to enter a complex situation of political ambiguity which is going to confuse the citizen."[336])

The Santer *Commission*, while admitting that the "difficulties experienced in ratifying the Treaty in certain countries showed how important it is to involve the national parliaments in the work of European integration"[337]), also wants to keep national parliaments active at the national level. It suggests that improvements of their traditional role be sought, "in accordance with the internal rules of each Member state, both in shaping the position of each Member state in the Council and in monitoring the implementation of Union decisions at national level."[338])

Within the *EP*, which is clearly the institution mainly affected by this debate on a second parliamentary chamber for the Union, the future role of national parliaments was a quite controversial matter. In the end, the general approach chosen was to advocate what was called an EP-national parliaments

---

[335]) Open letter to Mr. *Davis*, cited from Agence Europe, 16 February 1995, 2 f; stress in original.

[336]) Speech before the European Parliament's committee on institutional affairs, cited from Agence Europe, 25 February 1995, 2.

[337]) Commission Report, SEC(95) 731, 16.

[338]) Commission Report, SEC(95) 731, 17.

97

partnership in democratic control of EU matters[339]). Within the field of the so-called first pillar, this strategy aims at improved co-operation between equivalent parliamentary committees of the sixteen assemblies only, and not at giving any legislative role to the national parliamentarians. Furthermore, the EP requires opportunities for specialised organs of national parliaments to discuss major European proposals with their ministers prior to Council meetings (this latter proposal is obviously mainly directed to the Member states because it concerns an internal matter). Outside the first pillar, however, the EP wants to see democratic accountability "shared between both the EP and national parliaments"[340]). This aims at abolishing "grey areas" of the Union's powers in which neither the EP nor the national parliaments have any power of control so far[341]), and builds on a rather realist expectation of the future of the Union's pillar structure.

Within the academic input for the IGC, it is mainly the *European Constitutional Group* which has promoted the establishment of an additional parliamentary body, the "Chamber of Parliamentarians", consisting of representatives of the national parliaments in numbers close to the current weighted votes for qualified majority votes in the Council [ranging in this case from 13 to 3[342])]. The members should be chosen every fifth year by the Parliament of that Member state from amongst its members. This chamber would have to give its assent to any (association) treaty by the Council. Before voting on any bill, the chamber would review whether it falls within the powers delegated to the Union; whether there was any need for Community action and for regulations; and check costs and benefits[343]). By contrast, various expert contributions explicitly take a stance against direct and specific involvement of national parliamentarians at the level of European legislature:

The *FT Round Table* argues that a third chamber consisting of representatives of Member states' parliaments would further complicate the decision-

---

[339]) EP Resolution from 17. 5. 1995, PE 190.441, pt. 24.

[340]) EP Resolution from 17. 5. 1995, PE 190.441, pt. 3.iii.: It is suggested that "consultation of the EP should be obligatory if the Council adopts a common position or decision on 'joint action'. The Council should be obliged to provide information on such matters and arrangements should be made for such subjects to be treated confidentially".

[341]) See e.g. *Jean-Louis Bourlanges*, cited in Agence Europe, 26 November 1994, 3.

[342]) European Constitutional Group 1993, Article VII of the proposed constitution.

[343]) European Constitutional Group 1993, 2b, p. 7.

making process and "would be necessarily less effective than the EP because its members, like the ministers in the Council but without the support they get from their officials, would be part-timers whose mandate would be different and whose main attention would be engaged elsewhere."[344]) The Round Table sees the main "European" function of national MPs as ensuring proper accountability of their own ministers in the Council.

> "There has to be a balance between the right of Member states' representatives in the Council to use their own judgement and that of the parliaments from whom they derive their legitimacy to hold them accountable; and that balance can surely not be based on secrecy of the Council's legislative sessions and lack of knowledge among Members of Parliament."[345])

The second task of national MPs would, according to this view, be co-operation with MEPs in order to feed relevant concerns into the EP's legislative work. Therefore *joint standing committees of MPs and MEPs* are advocated to deal with matters such as fraud, the CFSP and JHA, where responsibilities are shared between the Union and the Member states[346]). Other proposals by the *FT Round Table* are that the Member state's Council delegations could include members of their parliaments (see already French proposals above), and that Member states' parliaments could be given the same access to the ECJ as the Union's institutions where the scope of competencies is disputed[347]).

Also *Ludlow/Ersbøll* dismiss the creation of a parliament of parliaments which would to their mind be either superfluous, but expensive, or effective and potentially stultifying[348]):

> "There is no question that European citizens would profit by more intelligent debate about EU issues in national parliaments, but the main checks and balances must nevertheless continue to be sought within the EU institutional system itself."[349])

---

[344]) Federal Trust Papers N° 3, 11 f.

[345]) Federal Trust Papers N° 3, 13.

[346]) Federal Trust Papers N° 3, 12.

[347]) Federal Trust Papers N° 3, 13.

[348]) *Ludlow/Ersbøll* (CEPS) 1995, 50.

[349]) *Ludlow/Ersbøll* (CEPS) 1995, 50.

They furthermore oppose the recently much-debated wider-spread application of the 'Danish system' (now also 'Austrian system'!) of strict parliamentary control over national ministers which could, in the end, undermine the
principle enshrined in Article 146 which insists that any member of the Council
must be in a position to commit his or her country.

After rejecting the idea of establishing a second parliamentary Chamber
representing national parliaments, because it would "provoke a direct conflict
with the EP and, if not accompanied by adequate measures, increase the duration of already cumbersome procedures"[350]), *'Justus Lipsius'*, the European bu-
reaucrat from within the Council building, suggests some 'softer' forms of
participation for national MPs. Thus, the Commission should systematically
request the opinion of national parliaments prior to adopting an important legislative initiative, for example via "green books"[351]). Governments should systematically organise consultation of their national Parliament before their representatives vote in the Council on legislative proposals. More frequent contacts should be organised between members of national parliaments and
MEPs[352]).

Last but not least, a most noteworthy input to the debate outlined above
should be mentioned: *COSAC*, the conference of EC bodies of national parliaments and the EP, rejected at its February 1995 meeting proposals to set up a
new chamber consisting of representatives of the national parliaments[353]).

• An Austrian Perspective

Clearly, no national set-up can be fully compared to the EU's institutional
system, and vice versa. However, the closest assimilation to national polities
such as the Austrian, would be to transform the Council of Ministers into a
weak federal chamber such as the Austrian "Bundesrat" which only possesses a
suspensory veto in general law-making. The prime legislator would then be the
European Parliament which might in turn decide on a European "government".

---

[350]) *'Justus Lipsius'* 1995, 37.

[351]) *'Justus Lipsius'* 1995, 36.

[352]) Without giving any deeper reasoning on it, 'Lipsius' also mentions the possible
variant of mixing the form of representation in the EP, by having half of its members elected
by direct universal suffrage and half elected by national parliaments among their members
(ibid.).

[353]) Commission Report, SEC(95) 731, 16.

Yet, most observers even within the expressly federalist camp would agree that such a mechanical transfer of national patterns is of limited pragmatic and functional potential. First, the real life of supranational politics simply countervails arguments to fully dismantle the Council — which would furthermore have to agree de facto on the relevant Treaty reforms under the label of an IGC. But second, it is clearly the governments who assume core functions in the national political systems on which the Union is built, even within what is legally in most countries the realm of the parliaments. De facto, West European countries are usually governed by a so-called "gubernative", i.e. the parties in government and the leading parliamentary majorities work together across the boundaries of what are thought to be "checks and balances". Consequently, the involvement of the governments indeed makes sense at the supranational level. This is true for functional reasons (they may rely on most expertise thanks to their bureaucracies), and for political arguments also. Clearly, the government is at the forefront of public debate and thus often regarded as a legitimate representative, especially in foreign policy, even though it is only indirectly legitimated. The latter fact, however, is a disadvantage compared to both national parliaments and the EP, and it became more salient as more decisions were transferred to the European level. For this reason, the EP has been significantly strengthened during the past years and its position should be further improved.

But still it may be argued that within the Union, the sub-federal units are over-represented, as for example compared to the representatives of the Austrian 'Länder' in the 'Bundesrat' which is by no means the prime legislative chamber in Austria. As it stands, the European Union consists of a directly legitimised Parliament (which is still not on an equal footing with the 'federal chamber', and in some areas practically excluded from the legislature) and an indirectly legitimated Council with representatives of the Member states. Is it thus a good idea to introduce another chamber, which would be equally directly legitimated, but by a national electorate according to strictly national procedures? In terms of legitimising the system, we consider this is not the case, as there already exists a relevant body. It might even produce a clash of powers between two directly elected sets of representatives, and further diffuse the EU system for the citizens[354].

---

[354]) As the former President of the EP argues, "this kind of involvement of national parliaments in European affairs (is) the opposite of what we need (...) [citizens] must be able to

But there are also practical reasons which speak against the French and the European Constitutional Group's idea of a second parliamentary chamber. As outlined above, the experience of double mandate of MEPs has clearly discarded the practice of double membership of parliamentarians. In this sense, control over details of EU legislation via national parliaments can at best be control in theory, but never effective control in practice. Furthermore, severe contradictions become evident as soon as questions concerning the working modus of such a new unit are reflected: If such a chamber was invited to take decisions by majority vote, the price for reinforced national control over EU affairs would be "reproducing in a parliamentary context the same problem that is faced by governments in the Council of Ministers. And how could each parliament delegate to a number of its members the right to vote on behalf of the parliament as a whole?"[355])

In comparison, the division of tasks between the two parliamentary layers (i.e. national and supranational) developed during the past years seems to fit into both a functional logic and a practical work schedule: let the Council members, which represent their countries at the European level, be under political control of their parliaments (who may, in fact, in a worst-case scenario even vote a motion of censure against it); but for European politics, the European parliamentarians are near at hand and better equipped to be a co-actor. From the Austrian viewpoint, a "second parliamentary" EU chamber consisting of national parliamentarians would somehow duplicate parliamentary influence: if Ministers, who represent the major European legislature, are held responsible by the 'Nationalrat', one may assume that the respective arguments and positions are well represented in the European decision-making system. Any direct involvement of Austrian parliamentarians would thus in essence be a duplication of that specific input — but not without costs in terms of money, decision-making speed, and complexity at the Euro-level. In contrast, a more reasonable option seems to encourage other member states to allow for similar scrutiny of their parliaments.

---

identify clearly what we in the EP are doing, what national parliaments are doing and the contribution that both sides are making to improving parliamentary control of executive decisions within the European Union" (*Hänsch* 1995, 6). Any additional parliamentary chamber would in no way improve efficiency, but constitute an additional layer of complexity within the institutional structure (*Hänsch* 1995, 4).

[355]) *Hänsch* 1995, 4.

Yet, could the adoption of a "Danish model" be digested by the European legislature involving up to 28 countries, without excessive costs in practical terms (i.e. delays, increasing probability of stalemates etc.)? This is hardly conceivable, particularly if we bear in mind the apparent difficulties already encountered by Austria, when, briefly after the accession to the Union, respective Council members were not given a mandate which was flexible enough to allow them to truly participate in the negotiating process. Consequently, an alternative approach might be more appropriate to serve as a general guideline. Here, we apply what may be called a *'principle of mutual non-interference'* of national and European political systems: The two layers of policy-making within the Union should be based on additionality (in the sense that each level complements the other) plus mutual co-operation, without ever having one layer structurally impeding on the effectiveness or democratic legitimacy of the other. Consequently, while national control over Council members is desirable and democratically necessary, it should not hamper the European policy process. However, also EU politics have to respect the national realm, and should even bear in mind possible problems arising there from. This is, for example, the case concerning Council votes. On several occasions, Council members were reportedly at odds with national preferences, or even mistaken or (mentally) absent during deliberations. In addition, countries have been bound on a long-term basis by options of representatives who would not be in office the next day (e.g. in the case of a successful national motion of censure). Even in such cases, no appeal-like procedure is provided. According to the rules of procedure of the Council, there is a "vote ad referendum" being practised. However, this again depends on the estimation of the relevant minister whether it might be appropriate to re-consult its national counterparts or parliament. Whenever a national minister deliberates outside this pattern, there is no way to overturn his action if it is not acceptable to national actors. Here, one option could be to pay tribute to national practice at the European level, and to provide for an "emergency break": if a government/minister is called out of office via a parliamentary motion of censure, his/her deliberations within the Council level should be open to re-consideration by the predecessor for a brief delay (e.g. two weeks). As the conditions for this will very rarely be met, no unacceptable complications for the Council should arise.

However, such a fall-back possibility would considerably facilitate parliamentary scrutiny at the national level: Parliaments would no longer have to use ex-ante means (i.e. overly strict negotiating mandates for their Ministers), but could rather rely on ex-post examination, because in crisis cases remedy would be available.

The problems of a generalisation of the Danish model by no means indicate that there is no recommendable way to improve the exercise of national parliamentary scrutiny over European affairs. In general, however, they concern internal national changes rather than Treaty amendments. This is true for improved information and transmission of documents via the national governments, for representation of MPs within national Council delegations (as is possible in the case of regional representatives since the Maastricht Treaty entered into force). It is even true for another of the above-mentioned improvements debated recently, i.e. joint committees of national and European parliaments, and the inclusion of relevant committee members of national parliaments in working groups preparing draft legislation at the European level. Also, as already proposed by Hänsch[356],' the exchange of information between national parliaments and the EP might be improved through a permanent presence of national parliaments in the EP in Brussels, for example via an "office of the parliaments".

g) Provisions Concerning the Courts

Even though the ECJ was complemented with a Court of First Instance (CFI) in 1987, the competencies of this court have been considerably increased recently, and the numbers of judges increased because of the 1995 enlargement, it has nevertheless become obvious that the judicial system of the Union cannot cope with the ever increasing demands. In this respect a number of proposals have been made. Obviously, there are two partly conflicting developments: First, further enlargement will lead to an increased number of judges. Given that some types of case should still be decided in the plenary, the question of a maximum size of a deliberative body is raised. Second, further enlargement (together with further integration and more awareness of the European dimension of the law), will equally lead to an increased number of cases. The first set of proposals therefore relates to the number of judges and the related organisational question of chambers in the ECJ.

'Justus Lipsius' describes the situation as follows:

---

[356] *Hänsch* 1995, 6; he also proposed the incorporation in any new or reformed Treaty of the Declaration on the national parliaments annexed to the Maastricht Treaty which might provide a symbolic backing for such efforts.

"The case is obvious that, for a jurisdiction which is often obliged by the rules imposed on it to judge in plenary meeting, the more judges you have, the less productivity you get, while, at the same time, an increase in the number of Member states increases the number of cases to be judged."[357])

'Lipsius' therefore suggests settling for a court of 15 members. If this should be considered politically inopportune, he proposes having one judge for each Member state, but dividing them into two "plenary" chambers with the President and one Vice-President participating in all judgements in order to ensure perfect consistency in case-law[358]). The CFI rarely judges in plenary meetings and would, because of ever rising numbers of cases, need more judges anyway.

Parliament is in favour of creating a larger number of specialised chambers[359]). The *ECJ* is of the opinion that the judicial structure of the Union should not be altered at the present stage of Union development. However, the Court seems to agree to specialised chambers in the long run, if integration was strengthened in specific areas and therefore the number of cases be increased[360], [361]).

A set of proposals concerning the terms of office have been made in connection with the idea of appointing the judges in a procedure involving the European Parliament (see above III.B.2.b). The *EP* proposes that Judges and Advocates-General should serve only one, non-renewable term of office of nine years[362]). The *Europäische Strukturkommission* suggests that the terms of office of ECJ judges be twelve years to prevent political pressure via re-appointment[363]). The *ECJ* is not opposed to a change of the term of office of its members (but strongly opposed to any involvement of the EP)[364]).

---

[357]) *'Justus Lipsius'* 1995, 28.

[358]) *'Justus Lipsius'* 1995, 29.

[359]) EP Resolution from 17. 5. 1995, PE 190.441, pt. 25.ii. and iii.

[360]) ECJ Report from May 1995, pt. 15.

[361]) Not directly connected to this discussion the *ECJ* also repeated its proposal already submitted to the last IGC that also the Advocates-General should be entitled to vote for the Presidency of the Court: ECJ Report from May 1995, pt. 18.

[362]) EP Resolution from 17. 5. 1995, PE 190.441, pt. 25.ii. and iii.

[363]) Europäische Strukturkommission 1994, 41.

[364]) ECJ Report from May 1995, pt. 17.

● An Austrian Perspective

The right to appoint judges to the European Courts is inalienable in principle for various reasons. The most important is the fact that it seems necessary to include all legal traditions in the Court's workings. Another important argument relates to the ECJ's function as a constitutional court: it seems essential for each political and legal entity of a quasi-federal community to have a voice in the institution that is in charge of settling constitutional disputes among its members. However, as has been outlined above, in case of further enlargement it seems to be necessary to limit the size of the ECJ in order to secure efficient deliberation in plenary sessions. Limiting the size obviously leads to the denial of the right to appoint a member of the Court for some countries.

The only conceivable solution seems to be a system of rotation on a temporary basis which could be as follows: every Member state proposes several candidates to be appointed in a European procedure (for the EP's participation see III.B.2.b). The distinction between judges of the ECJ and the CFI would be dropped. All appointed judges (e.g. two per Member state, i.e. today 30 judges) form a pool and elect the members of the different chambers of the CFI and of an ECJ whose size could be fixed at for example thirteen members. The election should be on a regular basis (e.g. every second year) in order to secure proper rotation among all members of the pool. In the event of an involvement of a Member state (whether it is the plaintiff, the defendant, or the country of the court asking for a preliminary ruling) which has no national in the ECJ at that time, it could be foreseen that one judge (e.g. the one who has reached the least votes) steps down and one of the nationals of that Member state joins the ECJ temporarily. A secondary effect of this system seems to be greater coherence between the different chambers and the two levels of Courts.

This system, however, does not in itself help to reduce the workload of the ECJ. Therefore it would have to be complemented with a new distribution of types of cases between the various chambers of the CFI and the ECJ. Considering that the ECJ should develop into a genuine *European constitutional court,* we propose restricting the ECJ's primary competence (as opposed to its secondary function as the court of appeal; see below) to truly constitutional matters. This would include opinions on Treaties with third countries; decisions on the division of competencies between the Member states and the EU; the correct application of decision-making rules; and the failure-to-act proceedings where there is a dispute between institutions and/or Member states. With respect to preliminary rulings the following system could be envisaged: a chamber of the CFI first receives the question. If it decides that it involves a (fundamental) question which has not been tackled by previous case law, it refers it to the ECJ, otherwise it hands down the preliminary ruling itself. Actions based on Article 173 ECT should be dealt with by the CFI unless the plaintiff is either an institution, or a Member state. For actions by individuals, the ECJ would be the court of appeal. There would be no appeal to the ECJ in competition cases: if DG IV was structured differently with a sort of politically controlled public prosecutor division, and a more independent quasi-judicial division, the CFI would already be the second instance in this regard. The appeal in cases brought by Union officials should be organised as follows: first, a single judge of the CFI would be in charge; and for appeals a chamber of the CFI of for example five judges, not including the first one. Thus the ECJ would not be involved in appeals of non-constitutional matters.

3. Procedural Matters

We shall now proceed to the proposals in the field of decision-making at the Union level: the right of initiative, which at the moment lies with the Commission; the reform of co-decision and the possible introduction of a two-chamber system with possibly a uniform decision-making procedure; the question of voting in the Council, particularly the abolishment of unanimity and the reform of qualified majority voting, as well as the issue of secrecy in the Council and the wider issue of transparency; the issue of enforcement and implementation, including the question of the EP's standing before the ECJ; and finally, the future role of comitology.

a) Right of Initiative

At national level, the right to propose legislation is not usually restricted to one actor. Not only the governments, but also committees of parliaments or groups of MPs, and sometimes even (large) groups of citizens, may make proposals which have to be considered by the legislature. In the context of the Union's decision-making procedures, in contrast, the right of initiative is in principle granted exclusively to the Commission. However, the Council and also the EP, since the Maastricht Treaty, can request a specific proposal from the Commission (Articles 152 and 138b ECT). So far, the full significance of this provision is yet to be tested, as the EP's two requests[365]) are still being considered by the Commission, who regards that "[s]uch requests do not require the Commission to put forward a proposal, but, under the code of conduct recently concluded with Parliament, the Commission will take the greatest possible account of them"[366]). The main difference to the national systems is thus that national MPs can draft a proposal for a law and bring it to a vote in their parliament, while both chambers of the European legislation can suggest a topic for legislation, but can neither force the Commission to actually take the idea on board[367]), nor have any influence on how the Commission formulates a relevant proposal (except for the fact that, theoretically, a motion of censure might be voted against the Commission by the EP). This speciality of the EC system is being increasingly debated with a view to the IGC.

The *Commission* itself, as one might expect, argues strongly in favour of preserving the exclusivity of its right of initiative, "if the inevitable confusion and lack of overall direction which would result from multiple competing sources of initiative is to be avoided"[368]).

As a surprise, compared to previous statements, the *EP's* report on the functioning of the Union with a view to the IGC 1996 suggests maintaining the Commission's right of initiative more or less unchanged[369]). However, the Parliament requests that Article 138b (2) ECT should be altered to require the Commission to respond to Parliament's initiatives[370]). Before that, the proposed Constitution of the *Herman Report* had distinguished between ordinary laws on the one hand, and constitutional laws on the other. The initiative for the latter could come from either the European Parliament, Council, Commission, or any Member state, while the first group could only be proposed by the Commission[371]).

---

[365]) Concerning preventing and remedying damage to the environment and making hotels safe against fire.

[366]) Commission Report, SEC(95) 731, 14.

[367]) Article 175 ECT on legal actions for failure to act seems to apply in principle. However, the relevant provisions (Articles 138b and 152 ECT) are probably not specific enough to create a legal obligation for the Commission.

[368]) Commission Report, SEC(95) 731, 3.

[369]) EP Resolution from 17. 5. 1995, PE 190.441, pt. 21.i.

[370]) EP Resolution from 17. 5. 1995, PE 190.441, pt. 23.vii.

[371]) Herman Report 1994, Article 32 of the proposed Constitution.

More recently, the French President of the National Assembly, *Seguin*, suggested that (only!) the Council share the power of initiative with the Commission[372]). Under the *European Constitutional Group's* proposed constitution, Commission, Council, and the two parliamentary chambers would each possess a right of initiative[373]).

- An Austrian Perspective

In order to locate the difficult question of "monopoly of initiative", some historical background information seems useful. This specific feature of the EC system was once created to provide some specialist, European-minded (critics might say "technocratic") counter-weight to the then exclusive legislative institution, i.e. the Council representing a "clearing house" for national interests. Subsequently, the European Parliament developed into a co-actor within EC legislation, which is furthermore directly legitimated by the European citizens. In consequence, its exclusion from at least equal footing with the Commission quite justifiably became a matter of debate.

On closer examination, the right of initiative has already developed since the EP gained more rights, and is now to a limited extent shared between Commission, Council and EP. It is no longer, as in former days, solely the Commission which may bring a halt to any project that, in its view, might harm the integration process in the long run, by withdrawing its proposal. Already, the co-decision and the assent procedures allow the EP to veto legislation which it considers inappropriate. Furthermore, the Commission's powers were somewhat restricted by the Maastricht Treaty, as it seems not to have the power to withdraw proposals once they have reached the stage of Conciliation Committee in the co-decision procedure. At that point, the EP's amendments may even be adopted by the Council without the unanimity which was formerly required for each and every departure from a Commission proposal[374]). Thus, more far-

---

[372]) Agence Europe, 8 December 1994, 5.

[373]) European Constitutional Group 1993, Article X, Sections 4 and 5 of the proposed Constitution.

[374]) Clearly, the provision that the Council may depart from a Commission proposal only by unanimity (Article 149a ECT) is inappropriate, along with increased powers of the EP and increased numbers of Council members. Without this being made explicit, it seems that proposals to abolish unanimity in the Council build on the assumption that the respective Commission powers are not replaced by any similar model (e.g., four-fifths *majority* instead of two-thirds whenever against Commission proposal) — which seems appropriate in our minds.

reaching reforms (particularly the explicit duty for the Commission to follow-up relevant proposals, subject to control by the ECJ) would not constitute a clear-cut departure from the existing model any more. On the other hand, the present state of power distribution may be considered illegitimate: Neither the Council nor the EP may force the Commission to initiate Union legislation on a specific topic — despite the fact that deciding what should be tackled by a legislature is a political question from which the democratically legitimated institutions should not be excluded.

Thus, a Treaty amendment with a view to strengthening, in particular, the EP's[375]) right to put issues on the political agenda, should be promoted. In that regard, however, secondary aspects should also be paid attention. At present, the EP is sometimes criticised for not having enough expertise for detailed legalistic work — a problem which it often shares with national parliaments, not least the Austrian. Clearly, one has to refer to the common knowledge that democracy is not for free, and thus ask for adequate means to be provided for the European legislature. Up to now, the legalistic preparation of legislative proposals, i.e. the drafting, has been exclusively managed by the Commission[376]). In fact, the way in which proposals are developed may be seen as one of the strengths of the EC system. In sharp contrast to frequent reproaches that the Union or rather the Commission's activities are overly centralised, there is an extensive pattern of consultation and mediation at the earliest stage of EC legislative action. The Commission manages a dense net of working groups which include representatives of national bureaucracies, as well as experts and lobbyists, whose knowledge is precious input for the European level polity. While similar practice is being conducted by the Council during the follow-up to Commission proposals, i.e. the negotiations between governments mostly within the working groups of COREPER, the EP is not yet used to comparable procedures, which might hamper its capacity of legalistic drafting. However, a combination of increased financial resources for the employment of qualified personal; improved status, which will certainly also bring about more prominent candidates; and possibly an elaboration of consultative procedures, which might for example include members of the national parliaments which work in

---

[375]) Quite obviously, in practice the Council is in that regard more powerful.

[376]) Except for the few areas where the Council may act without Commission proposal, and except for all amendments both Council and Parliament can propose.

the relevant fields[377]), and the Commission could clearly improve the status quo.

Last but not least it should be mentioned that the Austrian, as well as many other countries' constitutions, provide for the additional possibility of direct involvement of the citizens in the agenda setting process of the legislature. The Austrian popular initiative ('Volksbegehren') implies that when a policy initiative gets at least 100.000 signatures, it has to be considered by the Parliament. Considering the pertinent crisis of legitimacy of the European Union, a similar means might well be recommendable. What could possibly be a better symbol against reproached remoteness of the Union than giving the power to its citizens to get some matters debated by a legislature which includes both their directly elected representatives and their governments? Or to entitle them to even initiate a European-wide referendum process? If thresholds were adapted to fit into the larger polity, there would be no danger, in terms of efficiency, to be feared (see chapter III.B.1.d).

In a nutshell: From a specific Austrian viewpoint, the extension of the right of initiative to the EP, the Council, and possibly also the European citizens, seems highly recommendable. Without this, the European system would fall short compared to the successful national experience of having all three levels, i.e. parliament, government, and the people, contributing to the eminently political business of legislative agenda setting. The Commission's argument that giving up the exclusivity of the right of initiative would necessarily lead to confusion and lack of overall direction is not convincing: First, national experience does not reveal any such consequences. Second, there are enough competent and experienced politicians involved in the European legislature who would notice any deviation of initiatives from a reasonable path and, consequently, vote them down. Nothing suggests that only the Commission be in place to give the Union coherent policies.

---

[377]) This proposal is also being mentioned by many who want to improve the relationship between the EP and national parliament respectively some who want to give the national parliaments a role in European politics, see chapter III.B.2.f.2. It seems also recommendable to include both national MPs and MEPs from relevant committees in the working groups of the Commission.

b) Reform of Co-decision

As outlined above, the co-decision procedure worked surprisingly well according to the accounts of all three institutions involved (see chapter II.B.1). However, a number of further questions are being raised with a view to future democratic reforms of the European Union's procedures. We will group them under three major headings: first, establishment of a two-chamber-system; second, introduction of a uniform decision-making procedure for the Union; and third, proposals on the reform of specific details or certain stages of the co-decision procedure itself based on some months of experience.

(1) Introduction of a Two-Chamber-System?

Extending the field of application of Article 189b ECT to other areas of Union competence on the one hand, and amending the procedure in order to balance the respective powers of the Council and the EP, on the other, may be seen as steps towards a fully-fledged two-chamber-system within European legislation.

Quite obviously, such a development is the EP's main goal of the forthcoming IGC — despite the fact that the notion of a two-chamber-system is not being used. The suggested guideline for democratic reform at the IGC '96 is outlined as follows:

> "[T]he European Parliament should have equal status with the Council in all fields of EU legislation and budgetary competence."[378])

Looking at the following detailed proposals concerning amendments to Article 189b ECT[379]), we have to conclude that these changes, combined with the extension of the co-decision procedure to virtually all fields of Union activities (except for CFSP)[380]) virtually build up to a two-chamber system consisting of the Council as the representation of the Member states (quasi a 'European Senate') and the EP representing the European peoples (quasi a European House of Representatives). This follows the lines drawn by the former EP's *Herman Report*, under whose proposed Constitution Parliament and Council would have

---

[378]) EP Resolution from 17. 5. 1995, PE 190.441, pt. 23.iii.

[379]) EP Resolution from 17. 5. 1995, PE 190.441, pt. 30.

[380]) EP Resolution from 17. 5. 1995, PE 190.441, pt. 29.

been put on an equal footing, as they would both have had to pass each legislative act with different majorities according to the type of law[381]).

At the present stage of the debate it is hardly surprising that the two other major EC institutions, *Council* and *Commission*, have been reluctant vis-à-vis this far-reaching option (thus, they do not make any proposals in this regard). Among the many political statements by single governments or politicians, it was mainly the *German Bundesrat* who went in that direction by asking for joint decision-making powers for the EP whenever the Council decides by a majority[382]). This constitutes one specific version of the much-debated division of parliamentary control between the national and European level: whenever the national governments can — at least theoretically — be controlled by national parliaments, the latter should stay responsible, while the supranational EP should control in those cases where single national governments can be outvoted. The EP, in contrast, would clearly adhere to the more integrationist model, arguing that national parliaments are de facto pretty busy with the national agendas and have no means to fully overview European politics, so that the specifically elected European parliamentarians should be the responsible democratic co-actor in all European legislation.

In contrast, an alternative, pro-nationally oriented model is advocated by the *European Constitutional Group* who suggests a three-chamber-system, with the parliamentary side consisting of two bodies: the "Chamber of Parliamentarians" with representatives of the national parliaments, and the "Union Chamber", i.e. a smaller version of the directly elected EP. All three bodies would have to give their assent to any Union measure[383]). The problem of double workload as outlined above, however, is not taken into consideration by this Group, and the same is true for other arguments tabled within the debate on the involvement of national parliamentarians in supranational decision-making (see above III.B.2.f).

Two other expert contributions, by the Europäische Strukturkommission and '*Justus Lipsius*'[384]) respectively, answer the question of a two-chamber-system to the affirmative. Facing the fact that the Union has taken a number of

---

[381]) Herman Report 1994, Article 32 of the proposed Constitution.

[382]) Agence Europe, 1 April 1995, 3.

[383]) European Constitutional Group 1993, 2b, p. 10.

[384]) '*Justus Lipsius*' wants to see the co-decision procedure modified so that the EP be placed on an equal footing with the Council ('*Justus Lipsius*' 1995, 36 and 49).

important competencies from the Member states, the same standards in terms of democracy should apply to the supranational level according to the *Europäische Strukturkommission*. This relies on the consideration that the importance of democratic legitimacy grow along with the number and weight of decisions taken at a specific level. While the indirect democratic legitimacy via national elections of the governments represented in the Council of Ministers might have been sufficient in the early days of EEC integration, the Europäische Strukturkommission does not consider the increase of competencies for the EP within the Maastricht reforms to be sufficient[385]). Considering, on the other hand, the persisting lack of European social identity, the Europäische Strukturkommission considers that only a system of double representation could offer a satisfying base of legitimacy for the Union. A combination of European and national resources of legitimacy are accordingly suggested, crystallised in a two-chamber system. The Council and the EP should decide all essential European acts on an equal footing — thus combining both the democratic principle[386]) and the principle of participation of the lower levels within the multi-tiered system. No decision should be taken without the consent of either chamber[387]).

There is still another aspect with regard to the EP's role as part of a genuine two-chamber system: the *EP's standing before the ECJ* is only a minor issue compared with other demands concerning the role of the European Parliament, however, it has symbolic importance at least: The *EP* wants the "current anomalies" to be corrected by giving it, like the other institutions, the right to request the opinion of the ECJ on the compatibility with the Treaty of international agreements, the right to bring cases (not only in order to preserve its own prerogatives), and the right to be informed of requests for preliminary rulings that have been referred to the Court and to submit observations to them[388]). The *ECJ* replies to the EP's aspirations that it sees no technical difficulties but wonders if it would not make more sense to solve this range of problems politically without transferring them to the judicial level[389]).

---

[385]) Europäische Strukturkommission 1994, 32.

[386]) The EP has to be decisive because effective control of the European policy process via national Parliaments is seen to be de facto impossible.

[387]) Europäische Strukturkommission 1994, 34 ff.

[388]) EP Resolution from 17. 5. 1995, PE 190.441, pt. 23.v.

[389]) ECJ Report from May 1995, pt. 14.

(2) A Uniform Decision Making Procedure?

Ever since the original Rome Treaties entered into force, based on a comparatively simple decision-making model, the procedural rules became both more complicated and more numerous. New procedures include the complicated budget procedure; the co-operation, co-decision and assent procedures; specific provisions for economic and monetary union, common foreign and security policy, as well as justice and home affairs. Including all sub-variants, there are more then twenty different procedures in use[390]) and some are admittedly hard to understand in all details, even by insiders. In addition, the implementation procedures (i.e. the famous committee procedures nick-named "comitology") "do not operate with a particularly high degree of openness"[391]) (see below III.B.3.f).

According to the *Commission*'s report, additional weaknesses have become obvious: the continuing divergence between legislative procedures and the budgetary procedure[392]), and the lack of logic in the choice of the various procedures and the different fields of activity where they apply[393]). The Commission, furthermore, criticises sharply that, in the institutions' day-to-day business, the proliferation of procedures harms the internal operation of the Union, because it creates conflict over legal bases:

> "Institutions may tend to choose a particular legal base not because of the substance of the measure in question but because of the decision-making procedure which applies. Such conflicts slow down the

---

[390]) Commission Report, SEC(95) 731, 23.

[391]) According to the Commission Report, SEC(95) 731, Annex 8: 22 variants, according to the Council Report, SN 1823/95, Annex Vc: 16 variants.

[392]) Concerning the EC's Budgetary Procedure (which cannot be discussed in detail here), it should be mentioned that on 29 October 1993, an Inter-institutional Agreement on budgetary discipline and on the improvement of the budgetary procedure was concluded which provides for a revision of the EP's role therein within the IGC. Experts have suggested that the only legally and politically consistent solution was to expressly provide full consistency in the text of the Treaties between the budgetary and legislative powers of the EP: "in all cases where the EP is given a power of legislative co-decision, it has to be given an equivalent budgetary power; in the other cases, its budgetary and legislative powers must imperatively be compatible" ('*Justus Lipsius*', 1995, 33). See also EP Resolution from 17. 5. 1995, PE 190.441, pt. 34 ff.; Federal Trust Papers N° 3, p. 19 f.

[393]) Commission Report, SEC(95) 731, 23.

whole process and can lead to action in the Court of Justice, which should be avoided if at all possible."[394])

Accordingly, many have argued in recent times that for the sake of transparency and continuing citizens' support for the integration process, a simplification was indispensable. The most far-reaching proposal is thus, evidently, the introduction of one single legislative procedure, possibly applied with different majority requirements as is practised in the national political systems. However, the Commission itself is not very explicit in that regard: it advocates a "radical simplification" of legislative processes, and refers to the concept of a hierarchy of legislative acts (see below III.B.3.f)[395]). However, with respect to the second and third pillar of the European Union, the Commission is far from openly advocating uniform procedures. It rather puts forward the argument that concerning the CFSP, the EP "plays a role similar to that of national parliaments in relation to national foreign policy"[396]) — without mentioning the fact that national parliaments may dismiss national governments, and may *de iure* oppose government action by legislation, which is clearly not the case for the Parliament at the EU level. The EP may not even put a motion of censure to the Council. In contrast, the Commission argues that in the area of JHA, "questions (...) are likely to have a direct effect on individuals' basic rights and public freedoms", so that "they actually warrant a greater degree of parliamentary control especially where binding legal instruments are involved"[397]). According to the Commission, one uniform decision-making procedure could, at best, apply within the EC and the third pillar of the Union. The same has also been argued by the ESC[398]).

This line of reasoning is also followed by the *EP*, which in its Bourlanges/Martin report takes a pragmatic stance by not asking for full co-decision, but only consultation within the CFSP. Within the first pillar and JHA, however, the EP is a strong advocate for a uniform decision-making procedure in legislative matters: it wants the number of procedures to be cut to only three, with the co-decision procedure being at the heart with very limited scope

---

[394]) Commission Report, SEC(95) 731, 24.

[395]) Commission Report, SEC(95) 731, 24.

[396]) Commission Report, SEC(95) 731, 14.

[397]) Commission Report, SEC(95) 731, 14.

[398]) CES 273/95 fin, pt. I.5.9 and I.5.10.

for the other two forms (assent in 'constitutional matters' and consultation in the CFSP)[399]).

This view seems to be widely shared if we look at other contributions to the current reform debate. The *Federal Trust*, for instance, wants co-decision to apply to virtually all Community legislation. The assent procedure should be kept for Treaty amendments and revenue ceiling, while consultation is again suggested for the field of the CFSP[400]).

The *Europäische Strukturkommission*, too, considers simplification of procedures to be indispensable for any increase in legitimacy of the Union. These authors, however, do not suggest the introduction of a single procedure in general. In contrast, they elaborate a specific model whose eye-catching characteristic is indeed simplicity[401]): initiative by the Commission; where appropriate consultation of the Economic and Social Committee, as well as the Committee of the Regions; then adoption (with or without amendments) by the EP, and adoption in the Council. If the latter cannot arrive at the necessary majority[402]), a Conciliation Committee consisting of equal numbers of Council and Parliamentary representatives may search for a compromise solution to be adopted by both chambers.

Also the proposed Constitution of the *Herman Report* suggests a very simple uniform decision-making rule for all sorts of activities (except for intergovernmental co-operation in the field of foreign policy). The only variations provided for concern different types of legislative acts which would need different majorities in either institution to be adopted[403]).

While admitting that "complexity of procedures has become really excessive"[404]), *'Justus Lipsius'* is much less innovative and much more conservative with his proposal to extend the co-decision procedure only to those areas which are at present subject to the co-operation procedure under Article 189c

---

[399]) EP Resolution from 17. 5. 1995, PE 190.441, pt. 29. Justice and home affairs are not specifically tackled.

[400]) Federal Trust Papers N° 3, 19 f.

[401]) Europäische Strukturkommission 1994, 35.

[402]) There is no further specification as to the quality of any Council 'majority' given.

[403]) Herman Report 1994, e.g. Article 20 of the proposed Constitution.

[404]) *'Justus Lipsius'* 1995, 46.

ECT[405]). Assent should be kept as an alternative modus, but no longer for legislative acts. Furthermore, '*Lipsius*' suggests that procedures to consult the EP should be more precise[406]).

The *European Constitutional Group*, in turn, does advocate a single uniform decision procedure — quite different however to the EP's or the Europäische Strukturkommission's ideas concerning details such as the EP's powers[407]).

(3) Specific Improvements to the Co-decision Procedure

Co-decision seems to be at the heart of many considerations about the future decision-making structure of the Union. Most advocate simplification and clarification of the rules as laid down in Article 189b ECT[408]). Some also make detailed proposals for changes to the co-decision rules.

The most elaborated proposals are to be found in *Parliament*'s resolution: the most important one is the elimination of the possibility for the Council to act unilaterally by reconfirming its Common Position in the event of conciliation failing to reach agreement[409]). If this possibility was dropped, the imbalance between Parliament's and Council's stand in the procedure would come to an end and Article 189b would merit its label 'co-decision'. Another EP proposal aims at simplifying and shortening the procedure in cases of obvious agreement between the two institutions: it should end where there is agreement at first reading stage[410]). Furthermore, the phase of 'intention to reject' should be eliminated and a simplified conciliation procedure introduced at the end of the first reading[411]). Also the Commission should have the power to propose and put to a vote, in the two delegations, a compromise between the conflicting positions[412]). Finally, the EP proposes harmonising both the majorities required for rejecting the final text (regardless of the results of conciliation) and the

---

[405]) '*Justus Lipsius*' 1995, 36.

[406]) '*Justus Lipsius*' 1995, 48.

[407]) See the Constitutional Group's ideas on a second parliamentary chamber, above.

[408]) E.g. the Commission Report, SEC(95) 731, 23.

[409]) EP Resolution from 17. 5. 1995, PE 190.441, pt. 30.vi.

[410]) EP Resolution from 17. 5. 1995, PE 190.441, pt. 30.i.

[411]) EP Resolution from 17. 5. 1995, PE 190.441, pt. 30.ii and iii.

[412]) EP Resolution from 17. 5. 1995, PE 190.441, pt. 30.iv.

deadlines for delivering the Common Position and the opinion in the first readings on draft legislation[413]).

The *FT Round Table* also presented a simplified co-decision procedure where both the Council and the EP have to approve a law to be passed[414]). Similar to the EP's proposals, one simplification would be to enact laws immediately if the Council accepts the amendments proposed by Parliament after its first reading, instead of proceeding with a second reading as at present[415]). Another improvement would be that the Parliament, if it decides neither to adopt nor amend the Council's Common Position, may convene the Conciliation Committee immediately after the first reading[416]).

A very specific proposal with respect to Article 189b ECT has been put forward by the *ESC.* It argues that "increased use of the co-decision procedure will require stronger consultative powers to meet society's expectations more fully"[417]). Confirming its readiness to perform its advisory duties also with regard to the EP, the ESC requests that it "be empowered, where appropriate, to contribute to the procedure laid down by Article 189b, at the second reading stage". More concretely, it wants to have the right to send the ESC rapporteur for the proposals dealt with to attend the Conciliation Committee's proceedings as an observer.

• An Austrian Perspective

Even though there are a series of other considerations and proposals in that respect (and this reports bears witness of this), the reform of the decision-making procedure of the Union is quite rightly at the heart of the discussion on how to end the democratic deficit. Austria is a democracy and a federation itself and has therefore a paramount interest in democratic reform of the Union. Doubts concerning the democratic legitimacy of the Union were quite prominent in the Austrian discourse leading up to the referendum on joining the EU. As has been argued above in extenso, the European Parliament should be the main transmitter of direct democratic legitimacy to the Union level since the

---

[413]) EP Resolution from 17. 5. 1995, PE 190.441, pt. 30.v. and 31.

[414]) Federal Trust Papers N° 3, Annex 3.

[415]) Federal Trust Papers N° 3, 19.

[416]) Federal Trust Papers N° 3, 19.

[417]) CES 273/95 fin, pt. II.2.

national parliaments have neither the capacity nor are better placed to control the supranational decision-making. Therefore, they can only play an *additional* role in controlling the national representatives in the Council. Furthermore, it has been established that enhancing the EP's powers does not mean taking further powers from national parliaments, but rather giving the EP the ability to scrutinise those powers that national parliaments have already ceded to the Council of Ministers and the Commission (see III.B.2.f). Having concluded this, further upgrading of the EP seems to be a logical and necessary, although not sufficient, step in the process of democratising the Union level.

From an Austrian perspective the relationship between the Austrian 'Nationalrat' (i.e. the first parliamentary chamber) and the 'Bundesrat' (i.e. the chamber of the 'Länder') might be considered of as a model for designing the Union's decision-making structure. The 'Bundesrat' participates in the federal legislation by confirming the decisions taken by the 'Nationalrat'. In cases of divergence, the 'Bundesrat' has the possibility to exercise a veto. As this veto has only suspensory force in most cases, the 'Nationalrat' may then insist on its decision. However, we have to bear in mind that the constitutionalising process which has led to the Austrian model, started in an historical situation of high centralisation after the previous monarchic system. In contrast, the EU is built in exactly the opposite way, starting out from a totally decentralized system which, furthermore, seeks, to some extent, to preserve its decentralized characteristics. Therefore, when compared to the Austrian situation, the relationship between Council and Parliament is almost reversed. Nevertheless, an appropriate compromise has to be found between the principles of democracy and federalism. For want of something more convincing, we suggest heading for the middle ground, i.e. equal weight for both institutions which represent the two partly conflicting principles.

In the previous chapters four main directions of reform were discussed; these can be summarised as follows:

(i.) Although recent experience with co-decision shows that the Parliament's weight has been increased considerably, there is still an in-built imbalance in the co-decision procedure as it stands. In order to put Parliament on an *equal footing* with the Council, the latter's right to insist on its Common Position after failure of the conciliation procedure should be either dropped, or equally granted to Parliament with respect to the position it has adopted during the second reading.

(ii.) The co-decision procedure should be *simplified* along the lines suggested by the cited contributions, according to the experiences gained during its one and a half years of application.

(iii.) The future ordinary legislative procedure should be *co-decision-like, rather than assent-like*. Co-decision underlines the equality of the two chambers representing the states and the population respectively by involving both in the decision-shaping, whereas assent involves Parliament only after the main decision has been shaped. However, in some cases the assent-procedure seems to be appropriate, especially in the field of foreign relations (as at most national levels, e.g. in Austria where parliament has to 'ratify' most international agreements).

(iv.) Finally, the future legislative procedure should be a *uniform* one, as at the national levels. It should apply to all Community affairs including EMU and JHA. In a first step, consultation could be conceived in the CFSP. However, as we have argued before (III.B.1.a.2), marginalising a democratic body in any field of Union activities is incompatible with the principles of democracy. Even at the national level, as in the case of Austria, parliament has the right to pass a law aiming at directing foreign policy if it is not satisfied with the way government carries out this policy. Furthermore, national governments are responsible to the respective parliamentary committee and have to report to it. These minimal requirements should at least be inserted in future CFSP rules.

c) Voting in the Council

Two issues with respect to voting in the Council of Ministers have been brought up by almost all authors included in this study: the possible abolition of unanimity (1) and the reform of qualified majority voting (2).

(1) Abolition of Unanimity Voting in the Council

The requirement of unanimity, although very important in the early stages of the European integration process (especially during the transition period, see Article 7 ECT, and informally after the so-called empty-chair crisis in the 1960s), has been in constant retreat since then. The adoption of the Single European Act marked the turning point when the so-called co-operation procedure was introduced in order to facilitate the Single Market legislation [Article 149 (2) EECT]. The Maastricht Treaty followed the same direction in general, but introduced unanimity with respect to some new activities[418]). Although unanimous decision-making can be seen as supranational in the wider European policy-making context (because of the supranational environment involving package deals, ECJ activism, horse-trading), it is still deemed to be the greatest safeguard for national sovereignty, especially for smaller states. However, as has been proved by the switch from unanimity voting according to Article 100 EECT, to qualified majority voting according to Article 100a EECT and the subsequent accelerated adoption of a series of measures of the Single Market programme, the unanimity requirement is one of the major obstacles concerning the lack of efficiency in the Union's legislative process. With a view to future enlargements to the East and South, the argument becomes even more pertinent since a Council with some 28 members is hardly efficient under the rules of unanimity.

Therefore, possible abolition of unanimity is even more widely debated now than ever. Some proposals are radical, some are very careful with respect to which areas should be opened to majority voting. The *Commission,* for instance, does not suggest a radical abolition of unanimity voting in the Council but points at the lack of a consistent underlying principle to indicate in which cases unanimity should be required. However, while listing the surprisingly long and very diverse matters still requiring unanimity voting[419]), it only refers to the special case of the combination of the co-decision procedure with the unanimity requirement in the fields of research and culture[420]), but does not explicitly detail further possible candidates for a change.

The *EP* is more radical in that respect: it suggests further extension of qualified majority and wants to see unanimity restricted to "areas of particular sensitivity" included in an exhaustive list: Treaty amendment, Article 235 ECT, and other "constitutional decisions" being enlargement, own resources, and uniform electoral system[421]). Also the *Europäische Strukturkommission* seems to imply that their uniform decision-making procedure works with majority voting in the Council[422]), but no further details are elaborated.

---

[418]) Especially in the fields of EMU, Culture, Industry, CFSP, JHA.

[419]) Annex 7 to Commission Report, SEC(95) 731.

[420]) Commission Report, SEC(95) 731, 24.

[421]) EP Resolution from 17. 5. 1995, PE 190.441, pt. 22.iii.

[422]) Europäische Strukturkommission 1994, 35: "Findet der Entwurf im Rat keine ausreichende Mehrheit....".

'Charlemagne' expects that the unanimity principle will persist for constitutional questions, (with the exception of some nominations such as the one of the Commission's President), for the CFSP and certain aspects of JHA[423]). Only R&D and environment policy might be shifted to majority voting without major difficulties, whereas in the field of social and fiscal policy major controversies should be expected. With respect to JHA, *'Charlemagne'* proposes that the part of activity "which consists in producing legal texts, namely in the field of free movement of persons"[424]) could be shifted to the first pillar and majority decision-making. There remains, however, a hard core of Union activities which could not be subject to majority voting[425]).

The *Guéna Report* adds that the requirement of a double majority within qualified majority voting (see below) would have the effect of creating the necessary conditions for an abolishment of unanimity requirements by lifting the handicap of a disproportionate weight of the smaller states. Furthermore, Guéna refers to the 'Luxembourg Compromise' which could still be invoked in cases of 'emergency'[426]). The Irish Foreign Minister *Dick Spring* obviously had the same idea when he said, in a speech on the future of integration on 22 May 1995[427]), that the unanimity requirement should be kept "when very fundamental national concerns are at stake" because "ending of the unanimity requirement could be counter-productive".

Some want to replace unanimity by a stronger but majority criterion in order to make the proposal less radical. For example the *FT Round Table* suggests that unanimity will be found increasingly impracticable in the future as the number of Member states continues to increase, so that a *very high qualified majority* may have to be devised for at least some decisions. With respect to some Community matters, such as the environment, development co-operation and the framework programmes for R&D, the Round Table already proposes at this stage transferral from unanimity to qualified majority voting[428]).

---

[423]) *'Charlemagne'*, October 1994, p. 60.

[424]) *'Charlemagne'*, October 1994, p. 61 (our translation).

[425]) *'Charlemagne'*, October 1994, p. 62 (no details given by these authors).

[426]) Guéna Report (French Senate) 1995, 18.

[427]) See Agence Europe, 24 May 1995, 3f.

[428]) Federal Trust Papers N° 3, 8.

With respect to the CFSP the Round Table calls for increased application of the qualified majority procedure to those areas that are not defence-related[429]).

Also *'Justus Lipsius'* suggests a *very strong qualified majority* in order to prevent paralyses, and impossible request of (simple) qualified majority in all areas[430]). VSM could for example mean four-fifths of the Member states and four-fifths of the total population, or even 90 % of each[431]). *'Lipsius'* suggests this VSM be applied in all cases where Commission proposals are changed by the Council (Article 149 ECT), concerning nominations and modification to the Treaties, and in most cases where the co-decision procedure now applies. But in very sensitive decisions such as within the CFSP or tax matters, a Council member could have the right to ask that the question be raised to the level of the European Council, "where, after discussion, this member should keep his right, either to oppose and prevent adoption of the act envisaged by the others, or to abstain and not be bound by this act which the other would be able to adopt"[432]). Already, during the last IGC on the Maastricht Treaty, *Germany* proposed a reinforced qualified majority, originally in the context of reforming EC social policy[433]).

The *European Constitutional Group* suggests that unanimity be reserved for changes in the constitutional framework and in voting rules. However, "for some constitutional decisions, such as accession, unanimity should be interpreted as *'quasi unanimity'* (i.e. the assent of mini-states with a population of 3m or less would not be needed for other Members to go ahead)"[434]). Such countries would be allocated half a vote (0.5 votes) in the Council. Should they "combine with another country in respect of the rotating Presidency, their votes or fractions will count towards the % threshold"[435]).

---

[429]) Federal Trust Papers N° 3, 30.

[430]) *'Justus Lipsius'* 1995, 27.

[431]) *'Justus Lipsius'* 1995, 39.

[432]) *'Justus Lipsius'* 1995, 40.

[433]) See *'Justus Lipsius'* 1995, 19.

[434]) European Constitutional Group 1993, 2b, p. 5; emphasis added.

[435]) European Constitutional Group 1993, 2c, p. 5.

(2) The Reform of Majority Voting

Majority voting will probably be a big issue in 1996: it was put on the agenda by the Council after considerable problems with the adaptation of the traditional system to the last enlargement. In some aspects, similar to the 'non-solution' which has been found in 1966 concerning the step from unanimity to majority voting (the so-called 'Luxembourg Compromise'), the European Council adopted a compromise concerning the lifting of the blocking minority. The so-called 'Ioannina Compromise' did solve the immediate problem of getting the necessary ratification of the adhesion treaties of two Member states, namely Great Britain and Spain, but left open the wider question of how to tackle the in-built problems of the weighting of the votes in the Council.

'Justus Lipsius' points at the fact that,

> "with successive enlargements, the relative weight of Member states having a more numerous population, under-rated from the beginning, has through the years been decreasing in the Council, contrary to democratic principles. The threshold of the populations which can be minoritised has increased from 30 % to 40 % (...)."[436]

We have to consider the fact that all prospective new Member states would be relatively small. *'Charlemagne'* discusses the continuation of the present weighting of votes in this case[437]. Based on two tables — which are well known since they have been presented in several papers since — he argues that mechanic extrapolation of the present system to a Union of 28 members would lead to consequences which are unacceptable in terms of democracy: first, a *minority* of 47 % of the European population could in principle constitute a qualified *majority* and, second, the smaller states of Eastern and Central Europe acting as a group could form a blocking minority[438].

There are two proposals for solving the problem, either by introducing the principle of 'double majority', or by re-weighting of the voting power in the Council:

(i.) A system of *double majority* has been suggested: to adopt a decision, it would be necessary to attain not only a majority of votes but also a majority of

---

[436] *'Justus Lipsius'* 1995, 38.

[437] *'Charlemagne'*, October 1994, p. 62 ff.

[438] *'Charlemagne'*, October 1994, p. 65.

the population (Bourlanges/Lamers proposal). The idea has found widespread support[439]). The *FT Round Table*'s recommendation is for a simple version of double majority: "a two thirds majority with present weighting, provided that the states forming the majority contain at least two-thirds of the union's population"[440]). *Ludlow/Ersbøll* suggest that the solution to the problem will be found "in the introduction of a parallel set of criteria which can be invoked in certain circumstances"[441]). They propose a 'population criterion' on which they do not elaborate any further, but underline that the appeal to it should be the exception of the rule and only available as a "last resort"[442]). *Spain* will clearly be promoting the bigger countries' interests within the IGC. A government paper therefore included the proposal (as already put forward during the Ioannina crises) to have the blocking minority reached by three countries that together have over 100 million inhabitants. However, Spain is well aware that this question might be the most difficult one of the whole IGC. Furthermore, the Spanish government asks whether one should not apply different rules to any new micro states such as Malta and Cyprus, compared to the founding member Luxembourg[443]).

The *Herman Report* proposes the principle of double majority of states and population *without weighting* of votes as a general rule[444]). Clearly, this gives the smaller states much more weight than at present.

In contrast, while acknowledging the need for adjusting the system of voting within the Council, the *European Parliament* opposes the principle of 'double majority' of States and population in its latest report, "as it is in the Parliament that population is represented", whereas the "Council represents States". In fact, Parliament goes even further in the opposite direction when it argues that the threshold for obtaining qualified majority should be lowered "from the very high level of 71 % that it is at present"[445]). *Luxembourg* is also opposed to introducing a double majority in the Council:

---

[439]) E.g. by the President of the French National Assembly, *Seguin*, Agence Europe, 8 December 1994, 5; *'Justus Lipsius'* 1995, 38; and the following footnotes:

[440]) Federal Trust Papers N° 3, 9.

[441]) *Ludlow/Ersbøll* (CEPS) 1995, 41.

[442]) *Ludlow/Ersbøll* (CEPS) 1995, 41.

[443]) Agence Europe, 11 March 1995, 5.

[444]) Herman Report 1994, Article 20 of the proposed Constitution.

[445]) EP Resolution from 17. 5. 1995, PE 190.441, pt. 22.iii.

"In all federal constitutions, the small states have a certain degree
of over-representation, such as in the United States' Senate. That is
what federalism is. If we wish to keep the peoples of the small
countries attached to the idea of Europe, we cannot take away their
acquired rights."[446])

(ii.) *'Charlemagne'* argues that the introduction of the proposal of a 'double
majority' of votes and population would overcome only the first paradox (a
minority of the European population could constitute a qualified majority). The
second one (a group of smaller states, e.g. of Eastern and Central Europe,
could form a blocking minority) remains to be tackled. The only possible solution therefore seems to be a re-weighting of the votes which could reduce the
present disproportion which favours the small countries. The re-weighting
would have to observe three guiding principles: (1) abolishing the anomaly that
a minority could impose itself on the majority; (2) the accumulated weight of
the new Member states should not be able to hinder progress of the Union; and
(3) the relations of the respective weights of the bigger states should not be put
indirectly into question[447]).

Equally, the *Europäische Strukturkommission* wants to see majorities in the
Council be adapted after widenings. It proposes two guiding principles: the
majorisation of the big members by the increasing number of small ones be
impossible; and, at the same time, interests of the small members be taken into
account[448]). Concerning the weighting, the *EP* wants the voting power to reflect the general size of the State but not strictly the proportion of the population[449]).

Not surprisingly, small countries have been coming forward against any
change of voting rules which might be to their detriment. For example, the
Prime Minister of *Luxembourg* argued that he could "recall no case in the history of the Community, neither in monetary affairs nor in fisheries, in which
one of the big countries, including Spain, was in the minority. This is a purely
academic debate (...) You do not need to tell me in a Treaty article that Luxembourg is a small country (...) The difference is that the big partners can say

---

[446]) Quotation from Agence Europe, 21 April 1995, 3.

[447]) *'Charlemagne'*, October 1994, p. 65.

[448]) Europäische Strukturkommission 1994, 38.

[449]) EP Resolution from 17. 5. 1995, PE 190.441, pt. 22.iii.

'no' three times a week and the small ones only once every five years"[450]). Equally, in his speech on the future of integration on 22 May 1995[451]), the Irish Foreign Minister *Dick Spring* said that Ireland does not see a real danger that the larger countries be outvoted in the Council.

In support of the smaller states, *Ludlow/Ersbøll* conclude that

> "[t]he bias in favour of small states in a Union of national states is in other words desirable in itself and should be enshrined in 'normal' procedures."[452])

Apart from the discussion of the issues of double majority and re-weighting, several other proposals have been put forward concerning qualified majority:

The *Herman Report* starts from the principle of unweighted votes in the Council and distinguishes between 'single majority', i.e. single majority of states provided that they represent the majority of the population; 'qualified majority', i.e. a two-thirds majority of states provided that they also represent a two-thirds majority of the population, and 'special qualified majority', which is not reached if either at least a quarter of states representing at least an eighth of the population, or an eighth of states representing at least a quarter of the population votes against[453]).

The *European Constitutional Group* proposes a framework of 'Quasi Unanimity', 'High Qualified Majority', 'Ordinary Qualified Majority', 'Simple Majority', and finally 'Qualified Minorities'. This system is suggested to provide asymmetrical decision-rules so that it be easier to reduce market barriers than to raise them[454]). A 'High Qualified Majority' is suggested for measures that "impose market restrictions" and measures in areas of high importance (e.g. foreign and security policy). It should consist of a four-fifths majority including each of the major Member states and no more than three others against [states with populations less than one percent of the EC total are excluded from the qualifying number of states[455])]. In contrast, the 'Ordinary

---

[450]) Quotation from Agence Europe, 21 April 1995, 3.

[451]) See Agence Europe, 24 May 1995, 3 f.

[452]) *Ludlow/Ersbøll* (CEPS) 1995, 41.

[453]) Herman Report 1994, Article 20 of the proposed Constitution.

[454]) European Constitutional Group 1993, 2b, p. 6.

[455]) European Constitutional Group 1993, 2a, p. 5.

Qualified Majority' would be constituted by the dual criteria of a two-thirds majority with no more than one major Member state being overruled and no more than five other Member states against[456]). So-called '*Qualified Minorities*' could initiate proposals for Union measures in the Council of Ministers or in either Chamber of the legislature. They would be constituted by at least three Member states (excluding those states whose populations are less than one percent of the EC in total) or by a 15 % vote in the two parliamentary Chambers[457]).

- An Austrian Perspective

The right to block the adoption of a certain piece of legislation, which might not meet higher Austrian standards and would therefore water down the level of protection, was an important argument during the debates preceding the referendum on adhesion in June 1994. Also the unanimity rule in the CFSP seemed to be necessary in order to uphold Austria's neutral status as a member of the Union[458]). Even the old and legally doubtful Luxembourg Compromise has been cited on numerous occasions in order to reassure sceptical citizens. Although the referendum finally endorsed the transferral of Austrian competencies to the Union, which acts by majority voting in many cases, the requirement of unanimity in others was certainly part of the underlying basis of the 'deal'. It might be questionable whether abolition of unanimity would affect the constitutional endorsement (and therefore require a new referendum); however, it would certainly affect the underlying political basis of the assent by the population to join the EU. The same is true for any considerable change of Austria's voting weight in the Council in cases of qualified majority voting: over-representation in the Council compared to the much larger Member states was also part of the deal.

---

[456]) The European Constitutional Group wants to see this applied for decisions which modify existing regulations without altering the level of regulation, and implementation of foreign policy measures. A 'simple majority' would there suffice for reduction of Community regulation and any measure that repatriates powers closer to the people.

[457]) European Constitutional Group 1993, 2a, p. 5.

[458]) However, in a protocol annexed to the Adhesion Treaty it is stipulated that the new Member states would not use their right to veto in the CFSP in an obstructing manner, i.e. regularly.

Be that as it may, we have to acknowledge the need for reform of voting in the Council with a view to further enlargement. The danger of complete deadlocks (as to unanimity requirements in a Union of more than twenty members) as well as the anomalies (as to qualified majority voting in a much larger Union after mechanical adaptation of the present key) cannot be denied and therefore call for sophisticated solutions.

Unanimity: The only way around the danger of stalemates caused by unanimity requirements seems to be its abolishment. It depends very much on the field of activity at stake whether this is feasible and/or desirable from the Austrian perspective. Looking at the Commission's listing of 55 (!) provisions requiring unanimity in the ECT, reveals a great potential for further reduction of the scope of the unanimity rule. It becomes quite clear that most of these provisions call for unanimity for no particular reason other than historical development (e.g. certain environmental provisions, the adoption of the framework research programme, the approximation of laws for the Common market where Article 100a is not applicable, etc.). In the few sensible areas where a sound justification clashes with the necessity to overcome present and potential stalemates, the idea of replacing the unanimity rule by a quasi-unanimity, i.e. something like the proposed VSM (90 % of votes and of population represented), could serve as a reasonable compromise.

However, two specific areas have to be dealt with separately from the Austrian viewpoint: the CFSP and constitutional issues.

As mentioned above, Austria clearly has an overriding interest in keeping its independence as regards foreign and security policy, at least as long as there is no well-functioning regional system of collective security, in the sense of the Charter of the United Nations, is in place. There are two options: either keeping the unanimity rule (which would have bad effects on the efficiency of the CFSP altogether), or allowing opt-outs from the implementation of measures based on majority decisions for those Member states which did not agree. However difficult to organise the latter option might be, it nevertheless seems to be the most appealing one from an Austrian point of view. From an optimistic perspective though we have to keep in mind that the whole arrangement would be necessary only for a transitional period until the reason for keeping the neutral status disappears due to a European system of collective security.

Further sensible questions relate to constitutional issues, where opt-outs are often not conceivable. Should unanimous decisions be necessary for future

Treaty/constitutional amendments? Clearly, the step away from a more treaty-like concept (with the Member states as the main actors disposing of veto powers) towards a more constitution-like concept (with the EU institutions being at the centre of further constitutional amendments) constitutes a decisive matter within any process of state-building. Looking at the political circumstances, it is rather doubtful whether the forthcoming IGC will be ready to go that far. However, a specifically high qualified majority for constitutional amendments seems to offer a sensible option. It would prevent frustration over stalemates for an overwhelming majority, while still ensuring that constitutional rules were not a matter of day-to-day change. But how to proceed with those members which do not agree? According to the specific matter at stake, two alternative strategies are appropriate. In cases such as new procedural rules or adhesions, the (very small) minority would have to accept the majority's decisions, as is common in state-like systems. Concerning decisions of further deepening with regard to policy areas, the 'outsiders' might be allowed to stay behind, i.e. to opt out, whereas the majority progresses with the agreed amendments. In any case, the minority might also be given the opportunity to leave the Union (see already the chapter on "Flexibility Within Unity", III.B.1.b).

Qualified majority: The question of weighting votes in supranational decision-making necessarily relates to various federal models. When thinking about a system of democratic and federal representation for the Union, the U.S. system constitutes inevitably a point of reference. But there are at least two major arguments to be made against simply copying this system in Europe. First, the U.S. model is unique and cannot be regarded as the natural answer to the problem of representation of states in a federation. The Austrian 'Bundesrat', the second chamber which represents the nine Austrian 'Länder' at the national level, is composed of unequal numbers of delegates of the Länder according to their population. The same is true for Germany, another federal republic within the Union. Second, the U.S. model was developed at a time when the United States were still composed of a small number of states which were much more similar by then. The situation in Europe is completely different: the Member states of the EC/EU have always been very unequal partners (the two extremes Luxembourg and Germany were already among the founding states), and they probably always will be.

In fact, the situation in the Union today is fundamentally different from the U.S. model: states *and* populations are represented in *all* major institutions:

every Member state has the right to appoint a Commissioner but the larger have two (see III.B.2.c); in Parliament, there is a considerable over-representation of the smaller and an under-representation of the larger countries (see III.B.2.a); and in the Council, the 'state element' is even stronger, but with qualified majority voting the size of the population comes back in.

Thus, there are two different models for the representation of states or the population within federations: paying tribute to differences in population only in one institution which is based on strictly proportionate representation (i.e. U.S. model, Congress), on the one hand; and respecting inequalities between the Member states in all institutions of a common polity (i.e. EC model), on the other hand. If we imagine a continuum between those two poles, there is no singular logic criterion where it is legitimate to place a specific federal system. It is a matter of history, power relations, and pragmatic choices rather than of applying federal or democratic principles as such. Therefore, a pragmatic approach seems to be as democratically sound as a call to approach the U.S. model. However, if there is a directly elected chamber, there is an additional criterion to be considered: the principle of proportionality. As we argued in chapter III.B.2.a, deviation from the principle of (equal) democratic representation is hard to justify if there is another chamber where states are represented as such and smaller states may thus be over-represented. Therefore, it seems sensible to stress the principle of one-person/one-vote for the EP.

Without proposing any details, we therefore come to the conclusion that re-weighting of the votes in the Council, and the combination of qualified majority voting with a population criterion should be addressed at the IGC in order to avoid the above-mentioned anomalies (East may outvote West; minority of population could constitute qualified majority). Yet, the Council's function is that of a chamber representing the states and therefore any reform should not abolish the distortion in favour of the smaller Member states in principle. The main sub-unit of the quasi-federation EU, the state, should retain its political role because it channels and mediates specific national, regional, and local interests — an indispensable function within the contemporary European polity (see also III.B.2.e).

d) Secrecy in the Council and the Wider Issue of Transparency

One of the main arguments in the debate on the democratic deficit of the Union has for a long time been the fact that the European legislature acts in secrecy: Until very recently, no Council meetings were open to the public, neither were the results of Council deliberations. The situation changed slightly after the debate on transparency was boosted in the aftermath of the ratification problems with the Maastricht Treaty. The Danish government, after having been confronted with a referendum opting against the Treaty revision, launched proposals to open meetings and publicise results of legislative votes, as well as the minutes of Council meetings. However, due to the reluctance of all other governments except the Dutch, reforms have not, so far, met expectations. According to the Council's new Rules of Procedure[459]), the meetings of the Council remain non-public in general; however, after a specific decision by unanimous vote, it is now possible that individual meetings be broadcast. The Council's statistics show that there were only 21 such public debates from January 1994 until March 1995, held on topics of general political perspectives (such as the working programme of each Presidency, as well as on some major topics of Community interest) or on important legislative proposals[460]). Furthermore, the Council started to systematically publish the voting results when it acted as a legislator[461]). Since a request by the British newspaper Financial Times to be informed of the existing number of qualified majority votes created considerable turmoil during summer 1994, the Secretariat of the Council also keeps a register of votes on legislation[462]). But still, the Council is an institution which prefers to keep politics behind closed doors. This is prominently shown in the fact that according to its rules of procedure[463]) the consultations of the Council are subject to secrecy. Consequently, there is no access to the minutes of the meetings of the major legislative actor at the European level. Due to the political positions of the Member states they contain, the minutes are deemed to be confidential documents. The Decision of 20 December 1993 concerning the public's access to Council documents[464]) gave rise to differing interpretations, with Denmark and the Netherlands arguing that there should at least be an appreciation of the secrecy of a requested Council document on a case-to-case basis. The other governments, however, opted for the

---

[459]) OJ 93/L 304/1 as amended by OJ 95/L 31/14.

[460]) See Annex III a of the Council's Report on the functioning of the TEU, SN 1821/95.

[461]) See Article 7 (5) of the Rules of Procedure and the Annex defining when the Council acts as a legislator.

[462]) See Agence Europe, 6 July 1994, 9.

[463]) See Article 5 (1).

[464]) OJ 93/L 340/41.

version that as soon as the communication of minutes is requested, refusal is automatic[465]). The former two governments' fight for a 'right of access' for the public was thus clearly lost so far. However, two new members with a deliberately open and transparent stance towards public access to information on political and administrative documents, i.e. Sweden and Finland, have entered the Union since. During the accession negotiations, they insisted on having a Protocol on increased transparency included in the Treaty. Thus, the matter is clearly not off the agenda — which is also expressed by the fact that the General Affairs Council recently called on the Committee of Permanent Representatives "to examine the conditions in which public access to the minutes of the meetings could be facilitated"[466]).

Also within the debates preceding the IGC 1996, many commentators have stressed the need for a change in attitude by the Council. For instance, the 1996 report by the *Commission* urges the Council to become more open in its legislative function[467]). It furthermore considers the abolition of the provision allowing for a Council decision against making voting outcomes public[468]). The *EP* goes even further and asks for an explicit statement of the 'principle of openness' in the Treaty: "where the Council is acting in its legislative capacity, its proceedings should be public and its agenda binding" and "[a]ll meetings on proposed legal acts are to be held in public unless a specific and duly justified exception is decided by a two-thirds majority"[469]). This is also the proposal of the *FT Round Table*, which acknowledges that decisive discussions might, if formal proceedings are public, take place elsewhere. Still it argues that "public formal sessions, at which ministers should present their grounds for supporting or opposing the law in question, would nevertheless provide a sounder basis for their accountability, and would be seen by the citizens to do so."[470])

Clearly, the matter of "bringing the Union closer to citizens and to achieve a maximum transparency" has always been a central aim of the Nordic countries in their approach to reform of the Union. For example the Swedish Minister of Justice, *Laila Freivalds*, suggested that the IGC consider introducing in

[465]) See e.g. Agence Europe, 25 May 1994, 12.

[466]) Agence Europe, 29 May 1995, 4.

[467]) Commission Report, SEC(95) 731, 35.

[468]) Commission Report, SEC(95) 731, 32.

[469]) EP Resolution from 17. 5. 1995, PE 190.441, pt. 22.i.

[470]) Federal Trust Papers N° 3, 11.

the Treaty framework a regime which would make it possible for the public to have access to documents held by the institutions, and that legal texts should be made more readable[471]). A "new right of all EU citizens to information on EU matters" also figures among the proposals of the *EP*[472]). The *Commission*, although acknowledging that the measures taken by it and the Council concerning access to documents "are still in their infancy" and that "it is too early to analyse in depth their effectiveness", argues that "it is clear that the principle of access to information is now undisputed. The basic instruments are in place, and a review of the code is planned after two years' experience."[473])

- An Austrian Perspective

Despite the fact that the relevant referendum produced a two-thirds majority for joining the Union in June 1994, Austrian politicians are currently confronted with a significant drop in public support for EC membership. Clearly, increased democracy and transparency at the supranational level are necessary conditions for significant improvement of public opinion.

Judging the interplay of European and national politics from a more structural angle, increased transparency seems indispensable to allow for efficient control of the supranational politics by national actors. This concerns parliaments as well as citizens. Thus, the Austrian Parliament was assigned the task of holding members of government responsible for their strategies in the EC Council. This was designed as a counterweight to the fact that, so far, the EP has not been granted co-decision in all areas where the Austrian Representative may be outvoted in the Council. Via variants of the so-called Danish model, several national systems try to uphold the principle that there should be some parliamentary scrutiny over all areas of EC-legislation. However, this is hampered by several difficulties[474]), one being that quite obviously detailed information on the agenda and negotiations at the Council level are indispensable. Because effective political control can clearly not be based solely on insider in-

---

[471]) Agence Europe, 10 April 1995, 3.

[472]) EP Resolution from 17. 5. 1995, PE 190.441, pt. 7.

[473]) Commission Report, SEC(95) 731, 89.

[474]) The major being that in fact the many meetings and complex decisions at the Euro-level cannot be effectively controlled by national actors which are already busy according to the national agenda and have no means of participating in any back-stage business in the supranational arena; see the chapter on national parliaments, III.B.2.f.

formation given by the subject of control (i.e. the Austrian minister who informs Parliament on Council debates), more transparency and especially access to the Council minutes and political statements annexed to them is crucial.

Second, European politics have gained more importance within all legislation which is binding on citizens of EU Member states. Thus, it seems indispensable that information on European decision-making be of the same quality as at the national level, if Europeanisation is not meant to lead to blurring of politics and thus produce protest. Furthermore, it is generally acknowledged that the Council of Ministers relies on a specific form of legitimacy, based on general elections and government formation within the Member states. As participation in the work of the EC Council has become increasingly important within the activities of any national government, it should accordingly not be kept away from public scrutiny. Logically, policy options at the European level will become a significant part of the political agenda of the Austrian government. Consequently, the citizens will sooner or later have to include European policy perspectives in their elective behaviour at the national level, and therefore want to be informed on such matters. Thus, the line of reasoning of any Austrian minister within the Council, such as his external environment in terms of the other governments' options, has to be known by national actors if policy-making in the European multi-level system is not meant to be de-legitimised in the longer run.

From this perspective, only a strong attitude in favour of increasing transparency can be recommended. The Council's minutes have to be made public in the same way as, unquestionably, the minutes of any legislature at the national level and the other chamber at the European level are. Clearly, there is need for negotiations behind the scenes (as there is in national parliaments). However, this must not lead to any political arguments or even to a voting behaviour which could not be explained to the public.

e) Implementation of European Law

When outlining the preferences of the French Council presidency during the first half of 1995, Foreign Minister *Juppé* stressed the necessity of an "in-depth control of the application of Community law in all Member states. This will lead us to proposing stronger mechanisms to deal with any violations"[475]). That

---

[475]) Agence Europe, 30 December 1994, 2.

refers to a well-known problem which it might, in the end, not be possible to solve without changes in the Treaty bases by the IGC:

> "[T]he EU is (...) almost entirely dependent on its Member states and on their legislative, executive, administrative and judicial authorities, first for inspiring and second for applying and controlling the implementation of the rules which it adopts."[476])

Thus, the Union has not been attributed sufficient means to control the application of its laws but is in contrast dependent on the help of those responsible at the national level — who might in fact sometimes even have a financial or political interest in the absence of strict control. The matter becomes ever more important within the debates on EC reform as anger about frequent breaches of European law (which are partly regarded as distortions of competition) rises, particularly among some governments. Most prominently, the British have voiced that they indeed see a need for reform. This might also develop into a strategically significant fact as it may well be the prime area where the British government is interested in any significant output of the IGC[477]). The problem finally culminates in the question of how to effectively fight against fraud to the detriment of the Community budget, which is not only costly but also heavily criticised by the wider public and thus harms the social legitimacy of European integration.

Confronted with concerns of taxpayers, Member states and Community institutions, that fraud be combated more vigorously, the TEU expressly assimilated the EC's financial interests to national interests, requiring the Member states to take the same protective measures as they take for their own interests, for example in their criminal law. However, the *Commission* report on the operation of the TEU points at the fact that the "new legal weapons" concerning the fight against fraud "hardly measure up" with the substantial interests at stake:

> "The efficient protection of the Community's financial interests requires an appropriate system of administrative and criminal controls and penalties in the Member states. Two proposals have been put

---

[476]) *'Justus Lipsius'* 1995, 5.

[477]) *Major* wants to make European rules more binding for all members in the field of implementation of EC law and fight against fraud (Agence Europe, 30 January 1995, 7). See also statement of the British representative in the reflection group, *Davis*, in Agence Europe, 18 February 1995, 4.

forward — one for a regulation on administrative controls and penalties, and the other for a convention on criminal penalties. Neither has yet been adopted"[478]).

As the chief explanation for the stalemates in the enactment of anti-fraud measures, the Commission points at the "paradox" of the necessity of unanimity in the Council, which also threatens to dilute the impact of proposed measures[479]). Second, power and accountability obviously do not go together because the Commission alone is liable in respect of budget execution, whereas the management of appropriations is often decentralised (e.g. CAP, structural funds). The Commission therefore urgently asks for extension of the Union's limited legal bases and instruments for fighting against fraud.

The *EP* even elaborated general guidelines for this area. It wants Treaty amendments in order to permit wider-ranging investigation rights (e.g. in a reinforced Article 138c ECT) and dissuasive penal and administrative sanctions to be imposed at the EU level. It advocates a new legal basis for directives with a view to harmonising the relevant penal law, "specifically obliging Member states to apply effective, proportionate, harmonised and deterrent penalties for breach of Community law."[480]) Independent agencies and other organisations entrusted with EU tasks should act within a framework which ensures proper co-ordination and control at the EU level[481]). The EP also asks for increased accountability of the EIB by means of judicial review by the ECJ; the competence of the Court of Auditors to monitor; and a reporting requirement to Parliament and Council[482]).

Several expert reports follow that reasoning to strengthen Union powers. For example, the *FT Round Table* states that "[e]ach government should be required to stipulate how it will carry out its share of the implementation of Community laws and policies. The Commission should have stronger powers to investigate suspected failure of implementation, to check lax financial con-

---

[478]) Commission Report, SEC(95) 731, 27.

[479]) Commission Report, SEC(95) 731, 27.

[480]) EP Resolution from 17. 5. 1995, PE 190.441, pt. 36.

[481]) EP Resolution from 17. 5. 1995, PE 190.441, pt. 37.

[482]) EP Resolution from 17. 5. 1995, PE 190.441, pt. 38.

trol by Member states in spending Community money, and, where fraud is detected, to bring criminal charges."[483])

Another point of criticism within the sphere of enforcement of European law is the fact that Article L TEU excluded both the CFSP and justice and home affairs (second and third pillars) from the scrutiny of the ECJ. The *Commission* regrets this because thus

> "neither the European Parliament nor the Commission can enforce their rights to be consulted, informed or fully associated, as the case may be. Moreover, neither the Member states nor the institutions can act to secure compliance with obligations imposed by decisions that have been taken."[484])

- An Austrian Perspective

Within the wider area of implementation of European law, four specific problems may be detected: difficulties within control of implementation and follow-up within the Member states of legal acts originating at the Euro-level; the question of sanctions for breach of EC law; the increasingly urgent fight against fraud to the detriment of the EC budget; and the control of Union primary law by the ECJ.

The first problem is prominently a matter of improving the Commission's staff and investigative competencies, as it is currently simply disproportionate if compared to the immense task of following up all complaints or hints concerning non-implementation in the Member states. Concerning effective sanctions for breach of EC law, it seems that steps are recommendable at three levels: if Member states do not fulfil their obligations to transpose Directives, the relevant provision of the Maastricht Treaty allowing for penalties to be imposed should be activated [Article 171 (2) ECT was never used so far]. In contrast, a Treaty amendment might be necessary to clarify the Union's right to approximate laws with a view to ensuring proper sanctions be imposed at the Member state level for cases of breach of law which originated at the EC level (e.g. if a Regulation is not respected by non-state actors). The same is true concerning powers for the Commission to fight against fraud: This matter should for the sake of efficiency not be left to the relevant government or re-

---

[483]) Federal Trust Papers N° 3, 24 f.
[484]) SEC(95) 731, 26.

gional unit alone. As far as EC institutions' rights or Member states' obligations under the second and third pillars cannot be enforced under the Union Treaty, it is obviously a Treaty reform which should guarantee the control of the ECJ within all activities of the Union.

Austria has a strong tradition of the rule of law. From such a national perspective it is clearly recommendable that the Union, which now legislates and administrates instead of the nation state in many areas, should not fall short of legal security. Furthermore, non-implementation of common standards may often distort competition to the detriment of more "obedient" countries. Last but not least, it is also, in terms of social legitimacy of the Union, an urgent task to stop breaches of European law as well as fraud against EC finances.

f) Comitology and Hierarchy of Legislative Acts

The last IGC tried in vain to establish a hierarchy of European legislative acts. Thus, Article 189 ECT still contains a (non-exclusive) catalogue of legal acts without hierarchical order. Furthermore, both the Council (at times in co-operation with the EP) and the Commission may independently apply a number of them (directives, regulations and decisions). De facto, it became common to issue framework directives which provide for a series of further directives. Also, there is the long-standing practice to "confer on the Commission, in the acts which the Council adopts, powers for the implementation of the rules which the Council lays down" [Article 145 (3) ECT]. However, no specific legislative acts are provided for the stage of implementation of European legislation. The relevant Treaty provision only provides for the Council's option to "impose certain requirements in respect of the exercise" of the powers conferred to the Commission, or to "reserve the right, in specific cases, to exercise directly implementing powers itself" [Article 145 (3) ECT]. In practice, this provision gave birth to a dense net of about 200 committees of experts of the Member states which control the Commission's implementing measures. Within this "comitology" (so-called because of the lack of transparency), a number of variants have been developed with powers ranging from pure advisory functions of the relevant committee, up to veto powers [the latter apply for about 30 groups[485])].

---

485) Commission Report, SEC(95) 731, 22.

More recently, since the co-decision procedure came into existence, the EP has felt that the Council should no longer have the sole power to delegate or intervene in the task of implementing measures which were adopted jointly by the Council and the Parliament. As a sign of protest and disagreement with the Council, the EP for the first time rejected a proposal under co-decision at the third reading (Directive on voice telephony)! Obviously, the Council does not welcome the EP's struggle for participation: it harshly criticises the persistence of institutional conflicts since the TEU entered into force, due to the tendency of the EP to struggle for additional rights, especially in the field of comitology[486]). However, the EC institutions agreed on a modus vivendi in order "to avoid further cases of stalemate"[487]) in December 1994 — which is however only to be applied until the matter of comitology be reviewed at the 1996 IGC.

This adds to the Common Declaration N° 16, annexed to the Final Act of the Maastricht Treaty, which put the issue of eventually introducing a hierarchy of legislative acts on the agenda of the IGC '96. The main idea is to accelerate the decision-making speed for implementing measures or rather technical legislation by making them legally dependent on higher-ranking legislation.

In this respect, the *EP* proposes a new category of 'implementing acts', responsibility for which would lie with the Commission where so empowered by the legislative authority[488]). Accordingly, the existing 'comitology' procedures should be simplified so that only advisory committees would co-operate with the responsible Commission. However, both Council and Parliament should be informed about the decisions on 'implementing acts' and would have the right to reject the Commission's decisions and to call for new implementing measures or for full legislative procedures[489]). Similarly, the *FT Round Table* calls for quick introduction of a procedure similar to that of British Statutory Instruments, i.e. most Union implementing legislation would have the force of law when issued but might be annulled on request by either the Council or the EP within forty days. For some of the most significant acts, however, enactment would need approval by the EP[490]). The *Guéna Report* mentions the issue of a hierarchy of laws with a view to reducing the number and range of texts

---

[486]) Council Report, SN 1821/95, point 33.

[487]) Commission Report, SEC(95) 731, 22.

[488]) EP Resolution from 17. 5. 1995, PE 190.441, pt. 32.i.

[489]) EP Resolution from 17. 5. 1995, PE 190.441, pt. 32.ii.

[490]) Federal Trust Papers N° 3, 22 ff.

submitted to the European Parliament[491]). Interestingly, Guéna does not want to use the differentiation among more technical and fundamental rules in order to reduce the work of the Council, but only to concentrate (again) the work of the Parliament to the "normal functions of a parliament"[492]) (without any further explanation). While in principle welcoming the idea, *Ludlow/Ersbøll* nevertheless doubt whether the introduction of a hierarchy of EU laws will in reality significantly modify the operation of the EU system[493]). *'Justus Lipsius'* points at the problem of delimitation between the different categories of acts[494]), which was in fact one of the main reasons why the problem was not successfully tackled in 1991. The *ECJ* draws attention to the fact that the introduction of a hierarchy of legislative acts would have to have consequences for the system of legal actions, especially for the individual[495]).

- An Austrian Perspective

In Austria, so-called "Verordnungen" are one task of the government which is, within the legal limits of the relevant law, free in its actions. Political control is exercised by the Parliament in so far as it may vote a motion of censure or, more realistically, might change or make more explicit the respective law at any point in time. In contrast, the EC Council of Ministers has strong political influence at the respective realm of EC activity, a feature that has its origins in the outdated dualist model of EC legislation which involved only the Council and the Commission in a decisive role. Since the directly elected EP is meanwhile a co-actor in many legislative areas, it seems a logical development that it too should have equal powers within the control of implementing acts. Any system which guarantees effectiveness seems recommendable, especially the model of allowing for an ex-post political control by both the Council and the EP, while the Commission plus consultative committees elaborate the implementing acts. A nominal hierarchy of norms, as exists in many national systems like Austria, seems desirable yet not indispensable as long as a systematic and democratic procedural approach is chosen.

---

491) Guéna Report (French Senate) 1995, 22.

492) Guéna Report (French Senate) 1995, 23.

493) *Ludlow/Ersbøll* (CEPS) 1995, 52.

494) *'Justus Lipsius'* 1995, 47.

495) ECJ Report from May 1995, pt. 21.

IV. Summary of Our Proposals

Below we shall summarise our major conclusions concerning the debate on institutional reform of the European Union from an Austrian point of view. We suggest referring to the relevant chapters entitled 'An Austrian Perspective' in part III.B of the study for a more elaborate explanation of our reasoning (the numbering of the following list is identical with that of the sub-headings in part III.B).

1.a) *Should there be a European constitution?* A major task of the next IGC is to make the treaty framework more accessible and coherent. We suggest not sticking too much to the labels of 'constitution' or 'treaty' with respect to the final outcome of this endeavour. However, calling what will happen in 1996 'the drafting of a European Constitution' might well play an important role in getting the attention and support of the European citizens. Fundamental human and social rights should not be excluded from a text that aims at serving as a reference point for human identities. Merging at least the first and third pillars is strongly advisable. With respect to the CFSP, a uniform institutional framework with democratic and judicial control should be the aim, although different decision-making rules for extremely sensible areas (especially those relating to neutrality) could still be applicable (for more detail see p. 47).

1.b) *Flexibility within unity: variations in European integration?* A certain degree of flexibilisation seems unavoidable and might in some areas even bear uniting impact, allowing for innovations to be first tested among a few only. Whatever the specific model of increased flexibility then adopted, the main condition should be that there is a certain core of activities which all Member states share, clearly centred around the internal market. The so-called 'horizontal' policies such as social, environmental, and consumer policies have to be part of the inner core of common Union activities. A model of 'variable geometry' should be based on a single institutional framework and not accept any stepping back behind the present acquis communautaire (for more detail see p. 60).

1.c) *Division of competencies between EU and Member states:* Given the experience of restrictive use of EC competencies due to the political success of the 'principle of subsidiarity' during the past two years, one could argue that the project of a genuine 'Kompetenzkatalog' for the Union is not one of high priority. Nevertheless, the IGC should at least try to codify the division of competencies in order to make it more transparent for the uninitiated citizen who wants to read and understand what the European polity is all about. With a view to democracy and transparency, it seems advisable to sort out the political questions which are typically involved in deciding on the appropriate level of political action in a given policy field as far as possible at the IGC (for more detail see p. 65).

1.d) *European citizens and the Union:* A European-wide referendum on the outcome of the forthcoming IGC would have a legitimising effect upon the new Treaty/Constitution of the European Union. Furthermore, the possibility of a European-wide popular initiative would open up to the citizens the opportunity to make European policies their cause (for more detail see p. 68).

2.a) *Composition of the European Parliament:* Over-representation should be confined to the states' chamber (Council), whereas the principle of proportionality should be applied to the EP with the single exception of a minimum number of three MEPs per state (for more detail see p. 72).

2.b) *Major EC appointments (including judges) by the EP:* The directly elected representatives of the European citizens should at least be on an equal footing with the Council with regard to major appointments at the Union level. The most convincing model seems to give the Council the right to propose an extensive list of candidates (e.g. for the highest offices in the Court of Auditors, etc.), and the Parliament the power to choose from this list. Concerning the Commission, Parliament should have the right to elect the President, who then chooses his/her team, again from a list put forward by the Council. The whole Commission would finally be subject to hearings and a final vote in Parliament. Concerning the ECJ, the list of candidates might be established by a body composed of the most senior members of the bench in each Member state (for more detail see p. 76).

2.c) *Number of Commissioners:* One Commissioner for each Member state would clearly be the preferred option. If it should prove desirable to decrease numbers in the longer run, it seems at least important to stipulate that no country be excluded from having a Commissioner for too long a period, for example no longer than for one term of office (five years) (for more detail see p. 80).

2.d) *Presidency of the Council:* The many-fold problems of the current presidency system would be even more enhanced after future enlargement and would, therefore, have to be overcome by an innovative system. We propose

144

the formation of groups among the Member states, for example: the group of the largest states (at present: Germany, France, Great Britain, Italy, and Spain); the group of the medium sized states (at present: Belgium, Greece, Netherlands, Portugal, and Sweden); and the group of smaller states (at present: Denmark, Ireland, Luxembourg, Finland, and Austria). In the event of enlargement it might be necessary to build a fourth or even fifth group in order to secure balanced groups of approximately equal size. The groups, every eighteen months, elect one Member state which becomes their member of the team Presidency. The three (or four or five) members of the team distribute the 'portfolios', i.e. the leading responsibility and therefore the chairmanship in the individual Councils, among them by common accord. It is understood that the external representation is performed by this innovative Troika, normally under the leadership of the delegated member of the first group. As to the composition of the Council, delegating from each Member state always the respective specialised minister and the Minister for European Affairs could both improve internal co-ordination of the national representatives in the Council and co-ordination and coherence between the different functional Councils (for more detail see p. 86).

2.e) *The future of the Committee of the Regions:* Significant up-grading of the Committee of the Regions seems undesirable. Representation of regional interests should be channelled internally by the governments and mediated by their representatives in the Council (for more detail see p. 90).

2.f) *The relationship between the EU system and national parliaments:* The idea of a second parliamentary chamber consisting of national parliamentarians is to be dismissed for various reasons. Instead of adopting the 'Danish model' in all Member states, a *'principle of mutual non-interference'* of national and European political systems should be applied: The two layers of policy-making within the Union should be based on additionality (in the sense that each level complements the other), plus mutual co-operation, without ever having one layer structurally impeding on the effectiveness or democratic legitimacy of the other. One concrete measure in that respect would be a sort of 'emergency break': if a government/minister is called out of office via a parliamentary motion of censure, his/her deliberations within the Council should be open to reconsideration by the predecessor for a brief delay (e.g. two weeks) (for more detail see p. 100).

2.g) *Provisions concerning the Courts:* We propose a system of rotation on a temporary basis: every Member state proposes several candidates to be appointed in a European procedure. The distinction between judges of the ECJ and the CFI would be dropped. All appointed judges (e.g. two per Member state, i.e. today 30 judges) form a pool and elect the members of the different chambers of the CFI and of an ECJ whose size could be fixed at, for example, thirteen members. The election should be on a regular basis (e.g. every second year) in order to secure proper rotation among all members of the pool. In the event of an involvement of a Member state (whether it is the plaintiff, the defendant, or the country of the court asking for a preliminary ruling) which has no national in the ECJ at that time, it could be foreseen that one judge steps down and one of the nationals of that Member state joins the ECJ temporarily. This system would have to be complemented with a new distribution of types of cases between the various chambers of the CFI and the ECJ. Considering that the ECJ should develop into a genuine European constitutional court we propose restricting the ECJ's primary competence (as opposed to its secondary function as the court of appeal, see below) to truly constitutional matters (for more detail see p. 106).

3.a) *Right of initiative:* The extension of the right of initiative to the EP, the Council, and possibly also the European citizens, seems highly recommendable. Granting the right of initiative to the EP should be accompanied by increased financial means for the employment of qualified personnel and the elaboration of consultative procedures which might include members of the national parliaments who work in the relevant fields (for more detail see p. 109).

3.b) *Reform of co-decision:* In order to put Parliament on an equal footing with the Council, the latter's right to insist on its Common Position after failure of the conciliation procedure should be dropped (or, alternatively, equally granted to Parliament with respect to the position it has adopted during the second reading). The co-decision procedure should be simplified and turned into the single legislative procedure. It should apply to all Community affairs including EMU and JHA. In a first step, consultation could be conceived in the CFSP (for more detail see p. 119).

3.c) *Voting in the Council:* Unanimity should be abolished altogether, even with respect to the CFSP. However, in this area, opt-outs from the implementation of measures based on majority decisions should be allowed for those Member states which do not agree. Concerning 'constitutional' issues, unanimity should be replaced by a very high qualified majority requirement. Concerning reform of qualified majority, we came to the conclusion that re-weighting of the votes in the Council and the combination of qualified majority voting with a population criterion should be negotiated at the IGC, but only in so far as it is necessary to avoid the unacceptable anomalies in the event of further enlargement. However, any reform should not abolish the distortion in favour of the smaller Member states in principle (for more detail see p. 129).

3.d) *Secrecy in the Council and the wider issue of transparency:* The Council's minutes must be made public in the same way as the minutes of any legislature at the national level, and those of the other European chamber (for more detail see p. 135).

3.e) *Implementation of European law:* The Commission's staff and investigative competencies should be improved. The relevant provision of the Maastricht Treaty allowing for penalties to be imposed should be activated. In contrast, a Treaty amendment might be necessary to clarify the Union's right to approximate laws with a view to ensuring that proper sanctions be imposed at the Member state level for cases of breach of law which originated at the EC level. The same is true concerning powers for the Commission to fight against fraud. As far as EC institutions' rights or Member states' obligations under the second and third pillars cannot be enforced under the Union Treaty, a Treaty reform should guarantee the control of the ECJ within all activities of the Union (for more detail see p. 139).

3.f) *Comitology and hierarchy of legislative acts:* The EP should have equal powers within the control of implementing acts. Any system which guarantees effectiveness seems recommendable, particularly the model of allowing for an ex-post political control by both the Council and the EP, while the Commission plus consultative committees elaborate the implementing acts. A nominal hierarchy of norms seems desirable yet not indispensable as long as a systematic and democratic procedural approach is chosen (for more detail see p. 142).

V. Prospects for Democratic Reform of the European Union After 1996

> "Looking for such solutions does not raise only questions of a legal and technical nature, but also, and above all, political ones: to obtain more clarity and transparency necessitates clearer political choices."[496])

Having suggested a series of detailed 'solutions' from a specifically Austrian perspective in the previous chapters, we shall now turn to the basic lines and evolving environment in which the IGC's 'political choices' will be made (or evaded). As mentioned in the introductory chapter, there is still a long way to go: the conference will probably not be convened before late spring 1996 and not be finished before mid-1997. Any attempt to predict the possible outcome could therefore at best be courageous. However, course and contents of the ongoing reform debate as presented and analysed in this study already reveal some trends. We shall try to summarise them in a series of preliminary points:

• It has become clear that further efforts to tackle the traditional democratic deficit have to be made in order to meet the expectations of the European peoples. While it is obvious that national political systems cannot simply be transferred to the European level, even the Council of Ministers states that the democratic quality of European decisions has to be equivalent. Despite all arguments about the multifaceted notions of 'state' and 'federation', it is ever more obvious that the institutional and procedural set-up of the European Union fulfils in many respects the same functions as any federation. But while, in 'ordinary' federations, problems such as a stringent division of competencies between the upper and lower level, or especially the role of the states at the federal (i.e. supranational) level were solved in a systematic way at the very outset of the respective project, this is not yet true for the 'system sui generis' of the European Union. Because these problems become ever more pressing with the further progress of European integration, the next IGC will clearly have to focus on them. Therefore, the debate will undoubtedly be dominated by the tension between the two partly conflicting principles of 'democracy' and

---

[496]) *'Justus Lipsius'* 1995, 46·

'federalism', particularly concerning representation at the EU-level. Since these two principles are not totally compatible, there is no theoretical guideline of how to settle the dispute (e.g. should the size of population be represented in one or several of the institutions?). Therefore, we assume that pragmatic approaches within the IGC are not only highly probable, because of the very nature of international politics in general, but will often also be theoretically justifiable.

• Although there is obviously a great rhetorical awareness that the citizens cannot be left outside the process of shaping Europe, it remains to be seen if this commitment actually leads to any practical steps. So far, there is almost exclusively input to the debate which concerns the representative aspect of the emerging European democracy. In contrast, little or no particular attention has been paid to direct involvement of the citizens in the EU system. The most far-reaching idea which has been widely debated so far is a Union-wide referendum on the outcome of the IGC itself. Ideas involving public initiative processes or even referenda devices for single major policy matters, as sometimes presented by expert groups, have so far rarely been taken up at the political level.

• The starting positions of the Member states show considerable divergence concerning both procedural/institutional matters and questions of scope of common activities. Clearly, extremes will have to be put together at the IGC. Unfortunately, the conditions for compromise are problematic because of the continuing necessity to find consensus among as many as fifteen Member states now. In addition, there are several members in this club whose interest in significant outcomes might be limited: not only the United Kingdom is still very reluctant towards reforms, also for instance the newly elected French President seems not to be on the 'fast track' of European integration. It is thus very likely that the only way around potential stalemates will be some sort of flexible approach, leading to a model of 'variable geometry'. However, if the advocates of this model stick to their basic assumptions and initial positions, keeping a uniform institutional framework should be of high priority. Therefore, even making European integration more flexible does in fact not enhance prospects for profound institutional reform, as again compromises with the more reluctant Member states have to be found.

• However, the assessment of the co-decision procedure was much better than expected by many. There is little left to do in order to make it a procedure which fulfils both democratic, federal, and efficiency criteria. This fortunate starting situation enhances the chances for positive reform considerably, because no 'great visions' are needed but pure pragmatism may suffice. The situation will already be different with respect to the spreading of co-decision to virtually all policy areas, which is another major demand with a view towards a more democratic Union.

• With a view to another major task of the Conference: the design of a system which allows for increased flexibility without paying too high a price in terms of unity and European identity ('variable geometry'), the most important question will be the content of the 'noyau dur' of indispensable policies which all Member states would have to share. The case of social policy will again be a particular point on the agenda. It does not however seem likely that the present British government would make any concessions in this respect, since the relevant opt-out is a major political 'asset' of the Tory government within its confrontation with back-bench 'Euro-sceptics' in its own party. Taking into consideration the eminent interests of other Member states that this specific form of possible competitive advantage be out-ruled, and the strong opposition of the Commission and the Parliament to this opt-out, the issue may well serve as a dangerous stumbling block — as in the last IGC. As well as many other issues, the composition of the governments of single Member states during the IGC will be of outstanding importance here.

• Regarding the search for possible areas of consensus between all Member states, the problem of how to tackle the implementation gap and fraud against the Community budget gain singular prominence. Particularly when it comes to new powers for the Union, and more specifically the European Commission, this is the prime area of compromise to be detected at this stage.

To conclude, we expect a rather pragmatic approach to be chosen at the forthcoming Intergovernmental Conference — despite the various far-reaching ideas which have been published recently. However, if at least the major improvements presented with respect to the co-decision procedure could be transposed into a new Treaty; if co-operation was replaced by co-decision; and if a major effort was made in order to make the Treaty framework more coherent and accessible, the prospects of democracy at the European Union level appear significantly improved, indeed.

References

Remark: We list here the documents in the language we actually worked with. For an English translation of the titles, please refer to the text (and eventually to the footnotes there)!

Allais, Maurice, "L'Europe face à son avenir — Que faire?", édition Robert Laffont/Clément Juglar, Paris 1991.

Ausschuß der Regionen, "Stellungnahme zu der Revision des Vertrages über die Europäische Union", Bruxelles, CdR 136/95 (SP) HB/M/CW/R/ms, 21 April 1995.

CDU/CSU-Fraktion des Deutschen Bundestages, "Überlegungen zur europäischen Politik", Bonn 1. 9. 1994, N° 10793; an English version has been published in *Lamers*, "A German Agenda for the European Union", Federal Trust and Konrad Adenauer Stiftung, London 1994.

'Charlemagne', "L'Équilibre entre les États membres", in: Volume in honour of Niels Ersbøll, October 1994, 56-80.

Conseil des Ministres, "Projet de Rapport sur le Fonctionnement du Traité sur L'Union Européenne", SN 1821/95, 14 March 1995.

Economic and Social Committee, "The 1996 Intergovernmental Conference: The Role of the Economic and Social Committee. ESC Bureau Report, Brussels, 26 April 1995", CES 273/95 fin, 4 May 1995.

Europäischer Gerichtshof, "Bericht des Gerichtshofes über bestimmte Aspekte der Anwendung des Vertrages über die Europäische Union", Luxembourg, May 1995.

European Commission, "Report on the Operation of the Treaty on Europan Union", SEC(95) 731, 10 May 1995.

European Constitutional Group, "A Proposal for a European Constitution — A Report, December 1993.

European Parliament, "Resolution on the Functionning of the Treaty on European Union With a View to the 1996 Intergovernmental Conference — Implementation and Development of the Union", PE 190.441, 17 May 1995.

Federal Trust for Education and Research, "Building the Union: Reform of the Union. The Intergovernmental Conference of the European Union 1996", Federal Trust Papers N° 3, June 1995.

Gericht Erster Instanz, "Beitrag des Gerichts Erster Instanz im Hinblick auf die Regierungskonferenz 1996", Luxembourg, 17 May 1995.

Guéna, Yves, (rapporteur), Rapport d'information n° 224, deuxième session extraordinaire 1994-1995 du Sénat, sur "la réforme de 1996 des institutions de l'Union européenne".

Hänsch, Klaus, "On Relations Between the EP and National Parliaments", speech delivered in Brussels at the European Policy Forum on 23 January 1995, Europe Documents N° 1920/27 January 1995.

Herman, Fernand, (rapporteur) "Zweiter Bericht des Institutionellen Ausschusses über die Verfassung der Europäischen Union", PE 203.601/endg.2 - A3-0064/94, 9 February 1994.

Jacobs, Francis, "The European Parliament's Role in Nominating the Members of the Commission: First Steps Towards Parliamentary Government of U.S. Senate-Type Confirmation Hearings", paper prepared for the 4th Biennial International Conference of ECSA in Charelston, South Carolina, 11-14 May 1995.

'Justus Lipsius', "The 1996 IGC", in European Law Journal 3/1995 (pages cited from manuscript); also: Revue Trimestrielle de Droit européen 2/1995.

Ludlow, Peter/Ersbøll, Niels, "Towards 1996: The Agenda of the Intergovermental Conference", in CEPS Special Report N° 6 "Preparing for 1996 and a Larger European Union: Principles and Priorities", Brussels 1995, 1-61.

Major, John, "Europe: A Future That Works", manuscript of a speech delivered at the Univeristy of Leiden on 7 September 1994.

Miller, Gary, "Post-Maastricht Legislative Procedures: Is the Council 'Institutionally Challanged'?", paper presented to the 4th Biennial International Conference of ECSA in Charelston, South Carolina, 11-14 May 1995.

Neunreither, Karlheinz, "The European Parliament and Enlargement: From 1973 - 2000", paper presented to the 4th Biennial International Conference of ECSA in Charelston, South Carolina, 11-14 May 1995 1995.

Weidenfeld, Werner (ed.), "Europa '96. Reformprogramm für die Europäische Union. Strategien un Optionen für Europa. Erarbeitet von der Europäischen Strukturkommission", Verlag Bertelsmann Stiftung, Gütersloh 1994.

Abbreviations

B-VG	Bundes-Verfassungsgesetz (the Austrian Constitution)
CAP	Common Agricultural Policy
CDU/CSU	Christdemokratische Union/Christlichsoziale Union
CEPS	Centre for European Policy Studies
CFI	Court of First Instance
CFSP	Common Foreign and Security Policy
COM	Commission Documents
CoR	Committee of the Regions
COREPER	Comité des Représantants Pérmanents
COSAC	Conference of EC bodies of national parliaments and the EP
EC	European Community (-ies)
ECG	European Constitutional Group
ECJ	European Court of Justice
ECSC	European Community of Steel and Coal
ECT	European Community Treaty
EEC	European Economic Community
EECT	Treaty establishing the European Economic Community
EMU	Economic and Monetary Union
EP	European Parliament
ESC	Economic and Social Committee
EU	European Union
FT	Federal Trust
IGC	Intergovernmental Conference
JHA	Justice and Home Affairs
MEP	Member of European Parliament
MP	Member of Parliament
OJ	Official Journal of the European Communities
R&D	Research and Development
SEA	Single European Act
SEC	Commission Documents (sectoral)
TEU	Treaty on European Union
VSM	Very Strong Majority

Schriftenreihe des Forschungsinstituts für Europafragen

Band 1:
Österreichisches Wirtschaftsrecht und das Recht der EG. Hrsg von *Karl Korinek/Heinz Peter Rill*. Wien 1990, Verlag Orac. XXIV und 416 Seiten. (öS 1.290,-/DM 179,50/SFr 161,50)

Band 2:
Österreichisches Arbeitsrecht und das Recht der EG. Hrsg von *Ulrich Runggaldier*. Wien 1990, Verlag Orac. XIII und 492 Seiten. (öS 1.290,-/ DM 179,50/SFr 161,50)

Band 3:
Europäische Integration aus österreichischer Sicht. Wirtschafts-, sozial- und rechtswissenschaftliche Aspekte. Hrsg von *Stefan Griller/Eva Lavric/Reinhard Neck*. Wien 1991, Verlag Orac. XXIX und 477 Seiten. (öS 796,-/DM 111,-/SFr 99,50)

Band 4:
Europäischer Binnenmarkt und österreichisches Wirtschaftsverwaltungsrecht. Hrsg von *Heinz Peter Rill/Stefan Griller*. Wien 1991, Verlag Orac. XXIX und 455 Seiten.
(öS 760,-/DM 106,-SFr 95,-)

Band 5:
Binnenmarkteffekte. Stand und Defizite der österreichischen Integrationsforschung. Von *Stefan Griller/Alexander Egger/Martina Huber/Gabriele Tondl*. Wien 1991, Verlag Orac. XXII und 477 Seiten. (öS 796,-/ DM 111,-/SFr 99,50)

Band 6:
Nationale Vermarktungsregelungen und freier Warenverkehr. Untersuchung der Art. 30, 36 EWG-Vertrag mit einem Vergleich zu den Art. 13, 20 Freihandelsabkommen EWG - Österreich. Von *Florian Gibitz*. Wien 1991, Verlag Orac. XIV und 333 Seiten.
(öS 550,-/ DM 76,50/SFr 69,-)

Band 7:
Banken im Binnenmarkt. Hrsg von *Stefan Griller*. Wien 1992, Service Fachverlag. XLII und 1634 Seiten. (öS 1.680,-/DM 260,-/SFr 262,-)

Band 8:
Auf dem Weg zur Europäischen Wirtschafts- und Währungsunion? Das Für und Wider der Vereinbarungen von Maastricht. Hrsg von *Stefan Griller*. Wien 1993, Service Fachverlag. XVII und 269 Seiten. (öS 440,-/DM 66,-/SFr 67,70)

Band 9:
Die Kulturpolitik der EG. Welche Spielräume bleiben für die nationale, insbesondere die österreichische Kulturpolitik? Von *Stefan Griller*. Wien 1995, Service Fachverlag.

Band 10:
Das Lebensmittelrecht der Europäischen Union. Entstehung, Rechtsprechung, Sekundärrecht, nationale Handlungsspielräume. Von *Michael Nentwich*. Wien 1994, Service Fachverlag. XII und 403 Seiten. (öS 593,-/DM 88,-/SFr 87,50)

Band 11:
Privatrechtsverhältnisse und EU-Recht. Die horizontale Wirkung nicht umgesetzten EU-Rechts. Von *Andreas Zahradnik*. Wien 1995, Service Fachverlag.
(öS 345,-/DM 54,-/SFr 54,-)

Band 12:
The World Economy after the Uruguay Round. Hrsg von *Fritz Breuss*. Wien 1995, Service Fachverlag. XVII und 415 Seiten. (öS 540,-/DM 82,-/SFr 81,60)

This book is to be returned on or before
the last date stamped below.